COWBOY SONGS
AND OTHER FRONTIER BALLADS

* * *

What keeps the herd from running,
Stampeding far and wide?
The cowboy's long, low whistle,
And singing by their side.

* * *

COWBOY SONGS

AND OTHER FRONTIER BALLADS

COLLECTED BY

JOHN A. LOMAX, M. A.

THE UNIVERSITY OF TEXAS
SHELDON FELLOW FOR THE INVESTIGATION OF AMERICAN BALLADS,
HARVARD UNIVERSITY

WITH AN INTRODUCTION BY
BARRETT WENDELL

New York
THE MACMILLAN COMPANY
1930

To

MR. THEODORE ROOSEVELT

WHO WHILE PRESIDENT WAS NOT TOO BUSY TO
TURN ASIDE—CHEERFULLY AND EFFECTIVELY—
AND AID WORKERS IN THE FIELD OF AMERICAN
BALLADRY, THIS VOLUME IS GRATEFULLY
DEDICATED

Cheyenne
Aug 28th 1910

Dear Mr. Lomax,

You have done
a work emphatically worth doing
and one which should appeal
to the people of all our country, but
particularly to the people of the
west and southwest. Your subject
is not only exceedingly interesting to
the student of literature, but also to
the student of the general history of
the west. There is something very curious
in the reproduction here on this new
continent of essentially the conditions
of ballad-growth which obtained in
mediaeval England; including, by the way,
sympathy for the outlaw, Jesse James
taking the place of Robin Hood. Under
modern conditions however, the native ballad is
speedily killed by competition with the music
hall songs; the cowboys becoming ashamed to
sing the crude homespun ballads, in view of
what Owen Wister calls the "ill-smelling saloon

cleverness of the far less interesting compositions of the music-hall singers. It is therefore a work of real importance to preserve permanently this unwritten ballad literature of the back country and the frontier.

With all good wishes, I am

very truly yours
Theodore Roosevelt

CONTENTS

Contents

Contents

xi

Contents

Contents

INTRODUCTION

It is now four or five years since my attention was called to the collection of native American ballads from the Southwest, already begun by Professor Lomax. At that time, he seemed hardly to appreciate their full value and importance. To my colleague, Professor G. L. Kittredge, probably the most eminent authority on folk-song in America, this value and importance appeared as indubitable as it appeared to me. We heartily joined in encouraging the work, as a real contribution both to literature and to learning. The present volume is the first published result of these efforts.

The value and importance of the work seems to me double. One phase of it is perhaps too highly special ever to be popular. Whoever has begun the inexhaustibly fascinating study of popular song and literature —of the nameless poetry which vigorously lives through the centuries — must be perplexed by the necessarily conjectural opinions concerning its origin and development held by various and disputing scholars. When songs were made in times and terms which for centuries have been not living facts but facts of remote history or tradition, it is impossible to be sure quite how they begun, and by quite what means they sifted through the centuries into the forms at last securely theirs, in the final rigidity of print. In this collection of American ballads, almost if not quite uniquely, it is possible to trace the precise manner in which songs and cycles of song — obviously analogous to those surviving from older and antique times — have come into being. The facts which are still available concerning the ballads of our own Southwest are such as should go far to prove, or to disprove, many of the theories advanced concerning the laws of literature as evinced in the ballads of the old world.

Such learned matter as this, however, is not so surely within my province, who have made no technical study of literary origins, as is the other consideration which made me feel, from my first knowledge of these ballads, that they are beyond dispute valuable and important. In the ballads of the old world, it is not historical or philological considerations which most readers care for. It is the wonderful, robust vividness of their artless yet supremely true utterance; it is the natural vigor of their surgent, unsophisticated human rhythm. It is the sense, derived one can hardly explain how, that here is expression straight from the heart of humanity; that here is something like the sturdy root from which the finer, though not always more lovely, flowers of polite literature have sprung. At times when we yearn for polite grace, ballads may seem rude; at times when polite grace seems tedious, sophisticated, corrupt, or mendacious, their very rudeness refreshes us with a new sense of brimming life. To compare the songs collected by Professor Lomax with the immortalities of olden time is doubtless like comparing the literature of America with that of all Europe together. Neither he nor any of us would pretend these verses to be of supreme power and beauty. None the less, they seem to me, and to many who have had a glimpse of them, sufficiently powerful, and near enough beauty, to give us some such wholesome and enduring pleasure as comes from work of this kind proved and acknowledged to be masterly.

What I mean may best be implied, perhaps, by a brief statement of fact. Four or five years ago, Professor Lomax, at my request, read some of these ballads to one of my classes at Harvard, then engaged in studying the literary history of America. From that hour to the present, the men who heard these verses, during the cheerless progress of a course of study, have constantly spoken of them and written of them, as of something sure to linger happily in memory. As such I commend them to all who care for the native poetry of America.

BARRETT WENDELL.

Nahant, Massachussetts,
July 11, 1910.

COLLECTOR'S NOTE

Out in the wild, far-away places of the big and still unpeopled west,— in the cañons along the Rocky Mountains, among the mining camps of Nevada and Montana, and on the remote cattle ranches of Texas, New Mexico, and Arizona,— yet survives the Anglo-Saxon ballad spirit that was active in secluded districts in England and Scotland even after the coming of Tennyson and Browning. This spirit is manifested both in the preservation of the English ballad and in the creation of local songs. Illiterate people, and people cut off from newspapers and books, isolated and lonely,— thrown back on primal resources for entertainment and for the expression of emotion,— utter themselves through somewhat the same character of songs as did their forefathers of perhaps a thousand years ago. In some such way have been made and preserved the cowboy songs and other frontier ballads contained in this volume. The songs represent the operation of instinct and tradition. They are chiefly interesting to the present generation, however, because of the light they throw on the conditions of pioneer life, and more particularly because of the information they contain concerning that unique and romantic figure in modern civilization, the American cowboy.

The profession of cow-punching, not yet a lost art in a group of big western states, reached its greatest prominence during the first two decades succeeding the Civil War. In Texas, for example, immense tracts of open range, covered with luxuriant grass, encouraged the raising of cattle. One person in many instances owned thousands. To care for the cattle during the winter season, to round them up in the spring and mark and brand the yearlings, and later to drive from Texas to Fort Dodge, Kansas, those ready for market, required large forces of men. The drive from Texas to Kansas came to be known as " going up the trail," for the cattle really made permanent, deep-cut trails across the otherwise trackless hills and plains of the long way. It also became the custom to take large herds of young steers from Texas as far north as Montana, where grass at certain seasons grew more luxuriant than in the south. Texas was the best breeding ground, while the climate and grass of Montana developed young cattle for the market.

A trip up the trail made a distinct break in the monotonous life of the big ranches, often situated hundreds of miles from where the conventions of society were observed. The ranch community consisted usually of the boss, the straw-boss, the cowboys proper, the horse wrangler, and the cook — often a negro. These men lived on terms of practical equality. Except in the case of the boss, there was little difference in the amounts paid each for his services. Society, then, was here reduced to its lowest terms. The work of the men, their daily experiences, their thoughts, their interests, were all in common. Such a community had necessarily to turn to itself for entertainment. Songs sprang up naturally, some of them tender and familiar lays of childhood, others original compositions, all genuine, however crude and unpolished. Whatever the most gifted man could produce must bear the criticism of the entire camp, and agree with the ideas of a group of men. In this sense, therefore, any song that came from such a group would be the joint product of a number of them, telling perhaps the story of some stampede they had all fought to turn, some crime in which they had all shared equally, some comrade's tragic death which they had all witnessed. The song-making did not cease as the men went up the trail. Indeed the songs were here utilized for very practical ends. Not only were sharp, rhythmic yells — sometimes beaten into verse — employed to stir up lagging cattle, but also during the long watches the night-guards, as they rode round and round the herd, improvised cattle lullabies which quieted the animals and soothed them to sleep. Some of the best of the so-called " dogie songs " seem to have been created for the purpose of preventing cattle stampedes,— such songs coming straight from the heart of the cowboy, speaking familiarly to his herd in the stillness of the night.

The long drives up the trail occupied months, and

called for sleepless vigilance and tireless activity both day and night. When at last a shipping point was reached, the cattle marketed or loaded on the cars, the cowboys were paid off. It is not surprising that the consequent relaxation led to reckless deeds. The music, the dancing, the click of the roulette ball in the saloons, invited; the lure of crimson lights was irresistible. Drunken orgies, reactions from months of toil, deprivation, and loneliness on the ranch and on the trail, brought to death many a temporarily crazed buckaroo. To match this dare-deviltry, a saloon man in one frontier town, as a sign for his business, with psychological ingenuity painted across the broad front of his building in big black letters this challenge to God, man, and the devil: *The Road to Ruin.* Down this road, with swift and eager footsteps, has trod many a pioneer viking of the West. Quick to resent an insult real or fancied, inflamed by unaccustomed drink, the ready pistol always at his side, the tricks of the professional gambler to provoke his sense of fair play, and finally his own wild recklessness to urge him on,— all these combined forces sometimes brought him into tragic conflict with another spirit equally heedless and daring. Not nearly so often, however, as one might suppose, did he die with his boots on. Many of the most wealthy and respected citizens now living in the border states served as cowboys before settling down to quiet domesticity.

A cow-camp in the seventies generally contained

several types of men. It was not unusual to find a negro who, because of his ability to handle wild horses or because of his skill with a lasso, had been promoted from the chuck-wagon to a place in the ranks of the cowboys. Another familiar figure was the adventurous younger son of some British family, through whom perhaps became current the English ballads found in the West. Furthermore, so considerable was the number of men who had fled from the States because of grave imprudence or crime, it was bad form to inquire too closely about a person's real name or where he came from. Most cowboys, however, were bold young spirits who emigrated to the West for the same reason that their ancestors had come across the seas. They loved roving; they loved freedom; they were pioneers by instinct; an impulse set their faces from the East, put the tang for roaming in their veins, and sent them ever, ever westward.

That the cowboy was brave has come to be axiomatic. If his life of isolation made him taciturn, it at the same time created a spirit of hospitality, primitive and hearty as that found in the mead-halls of Beowulf. He faced the wind and the rain, the snow of winter, the fearful dust-storms of alkali desert wastes, with the same uncomplaining quiet. Not all his work was on the ranch and the trail. To the cowboy, more than to the goldseekers, more than to Uncle Sam's soldiers, is due the conquest of the West. Along his winding cattle trails the

Collector's Note

Forty-Niners found their way to California. The
cowboy has fought back the Indians ever since ranch-
ing became a business and as long as Indians remained
to be fought. He played his part in winning the
great slice of territory that the United States took
away from Mexico. He has always been on the
skirmish line of civilization. Restless, fearless,
chivalric, elemental, he lived hard, shot quick and
true, and died with his face to his foe. Still much
misunderstood, he is often slandered, nearly always
caricatured, both by the press and by the stage. Perhaps these songs, coming direct from the cowboy's
experience, giving vent to his careless and his tender
emotions, will afford future generations a truer con-
ception of what he really was than is now possessed
by those who know him only through highly colored
romances.

The big ranches of the West are now being cut up
into small farms. The nester has come, and come to
stay. Gone is the buffalo, the Indian warwhoop, the
free grass of the open plain; — even the stinging
lizard, the horned frog, the centipede, the prairie
dog, the rattlesnake, are fast disappearing. Save
in some of the secluded valleys of southern New
Mexico, the old-time round-up is no more; the trails
to Kansas and to Montana have become grass-grown
or lost in fields of waving grain; the maverick steer,
the regal longhorn, has been supplanted by his un-
poetic but more beefy and profitable Polled Angus,
Durham, and Hereford cousins from across the seas.

The changing and romantic West of the early days lives mainly in story and in song. The last figure to vanish is the cowboy, the animating spirit of the vanishing era. He sits his horse easily as he rides through a wide valley, enclosed by mountains, clad in the hazy purple of coming night,— with his face turned steadily down the long, long road, " the road that the sun goes down." Dauntless, reckless, without the unearthly purity of Sir Galahad though as gentle to a pure woman as King Arthur, he is truly a knight of the twentieth century. A vagrant puff of wind shakes a corner of the crimson hand-kerchief knotted loosely at his throat; the thud of his pony's feet mingling with the jingle of his spurs is borne back; and as the careless, gracious, lovable figure disappears over the divide, the breeze brings to the ears, faint and far yet cheery still, the refrain of a cowboy song:

Whoopee ti yi, git along, little dogies;
  It's my misfortune and none of your own.
Whoopee ti yi, git along, little dogies;
  For you know Wyoming will be your new home.

As for the songs of this collection, I have violated the ethics of ballad-gatherers, in a few instances, by selecting and putting together what seemed to be the best lines from different versions, all telling the same story. Frankly, the volume is meant to be popular. The songs have been arranged in some such hap-

hazard way as they were collected,— jotted down
on a table in the rear of saloons, scrawled on an
envelope while squatting about a campfire, caught
behind the scenes of a broncho-busting outfit.   Later,
it is hoped that enough interest will be aroused to
justify printing all the variants of these songs, ac-
companied by the music and such explanatory
notes as may be useful; the negro folk-songs, the
songs of the lumber jacks, the songs of the moun-
taineers, and the songs of the sea, already partially
collected, being included in the final publication.
The songs of this collection, never before in print,
as a rule have been taken down from oral recitation.
In only a few instances have I been able to discover the authorship of any song.   They seem to
have sprung up as quietly and mysteriously as does
the grass on the plains.   All have been popular with
the range riders, several being current all the way
from Texas to Montana, and quite as long as the
old Chisholm Trail stretching between these states.
Some of the songs the cowboy certainly composed;
all of them he sang.   Obviously, a number of the
most characteristic cannot be printed for general
circulation.   To paraphrase slightly what Sidney
Lanier said of Walt Whitman's poetry, they are raw
collops slashed from the rump of Nature, and never
mind the gristle.   Likewise some of the strong ad-
jectives and nouns have been softened,— Jonahed, as
George Meredith would have said.   There is, how-

ever, a Homeric quality about the cowboy's profanity and vulgarity that pleases rather than repulses. The broad sky under which he slept, the limitless plains over which he rode, the big, open, free life he lived near to Nature's breast, taught him simplicity, calm, directness. He spoke out plainly the impulses of his heart. But as yet so-called polite society is not quite willing to hear.

It is entirely impossible to acknowledge the assistance I have received from many persons. To Professors Barrett Wendell and G. L. Kittredge, of Harvard, I must gratefully acknowledge constant and generous encouragement. Messrs. Jeff Hanna, of Meridian, Texas; John B. Jones, a student of the Agricultural and Mechanical College of Texas; H. Knight, Sterling City, Texas; John Lang Sinclair, San Antonio; A. H. Belo & Co., Dallas; Tom Hight, of Mangum, Oklahoma; R. Bedichek, of Deming, N. M.; Benjamin Wyche, Librarian of the Carnegie Library, San Antonio; Mrs. M. B. Wight, of Ft. Thomas, Arizona; Dr. L. W. Payne, Jr., and Dr. Morgan Callaway, Jr., of the University of Texas; and my brother, R. C. Lomax, Austin; — have rendered me especially helpful service in furnishing material, for which I also render grateful thanks.

Among the negroes, rivermen, miners, soldiers, seamen, lumbermen, railroad men, and ranchmen of the United States and Canada there are many indigenous folk-songs not included in this volume. Of some of them I have traces, and I shall surely run them down. I beg the co-operation of all who are interested in this vital, however humble, expression of American literature.

J. A. L.

Deming, New Mexico,
August 8, 1910.

COWBOY SONGS
AND OTHER FRONTIER BALLADS

THE DYING COWBOY *

" O BURY me not on the lone prairie,"
These words came low and mournfully
From the pallid lips of a youth who lay
On his dying bed at the close of day.

He had wailed in pain till o'er his brow
Death's shadows fast were gathering now;
He thought of his home and his loved ones nigh
As the cowboys gathered to see him die.

" O bury me not on the lone prairie
Where the wild cayotes will howl o'er me,
In a narrow grave just six by three,
O bury me not on the lone prairie.

" In fancy I listen to the well known words
Of the free, wild winds and the song of the birds;
I think of home and the cottage in the bower
And the scenes I loved in my childhood's hour.

" It matters not, I've oft been told,
Where the body lies when the heart grows cold;
Yet grant, Oh grant this wish to me,
O bury me not on the lone prairie.

* In this song, as in several others, the chorus should come
in after each stanza. The arrangement followed has been adopted
to illustrate versions current in different sections.

3

" O then bury me not on the lone prairie,
In a narrow grave six foot by three,
Where the buffalo paws o'er a prairie sea,
O bury me not on the lone prairie.

" I've always wished to be laid when I died
In the little churchyard on the green hillside;
By my father's grave, there let mine be,
And bury me not on the lone prairie

" Let my death slumber be where my mother's
    prayer
And a sister's tear will mingle there,
Where my friends can come and weep o'er me;
O bury me not on the lone prairie.

" O bury me not on the lone prairie
In a narrow grave just six by three,
Where the buzzard waits and the wind blows free;
Then bury me not on the lone prairie.

" There is another whose tears may be shed
For one who lies on a prairie bed;
It pained me then and it pains me now; —
She has curled these locks, she has kissed this brow.

" These locks she has curled, shall the rattlesnake
    kiss?
This brow she has kissed, shall the cold grave press?

4

The Dying Cowboy

For the sake of the loved ones that will weep for me
O bury me not on the lone prairie.

> " O bury me not on the lone prairie
> Where the wild cayotes will howl o'er me,
> Where the buzzard beats and the wind goes free,
> O bury me not on the lone prairie.

" O bury me not," and his voice failed there,
But we took no heed of his dying prayer;
In a narrow grave just six by three
We buried him there on the lone prairie.

Where the dew-drops glow and the butterflies rest,
And the flowers bloom o'er the prairie's crest;
Where the wild cayote and winds sport free
On a wet saddle blanket lay a cowboy-ee.

> " O bury me not on the lone prairie
> Where the wild cayotes will howl o'er me,
> Where the rattlesnakes hiss and the crow flies free
> O bury me not on the lone prairie."

O we buried him there on the lone prairie
Where the wild rose blooms and the wind blows free,
O his pale young face nevermore to see,—
For we buried him there on the lone prairie.

Yes, we buried him there on the lone prairie
Where the owl all night hoots mournfully,

The Dying Cowboy

And the blizzard beats and the winds blow free
O'er his lowly grave on the lone prairie.

And the cowboys now as they roam the plain,—
For they marked the spot where his bones were
lain,—
Fling a handful of roses o'er his grave,
With a prayer to Him who his soul will save.

   "O bury me not on the lone prairie
   Where the wolves can howl and growl o'er me;
   Fling a handful of roses o'er my grave
   With a prayer to Him who my soul will save."

The Dying Cowboy

"O bu-ry me not on the lone prai-rie,"

These words came low.. and mourn-ful-ly...

From the pal-lid lips of a youth who lay

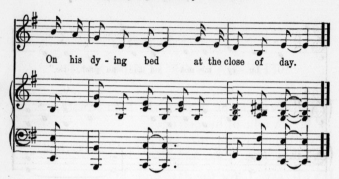

On his dy - ing bed   at the close of   day.

THE DAYS OF FORTY-NINE

W^E are gazing now on old Tom Moore,
  A relic of bygone days;
'Tis a bummer, too, they call me now,
 But what cares I for praise?
It's oft, says I, for the days gone by,
 It's oft do I repine
For the days of old when we dug out the gold
 In those days of Forty-Nine.

My comrades they all loved me well,
 The jolly, saucy crew;
A few hard cases, I will admit,
 Though they were brave and true.
Whatever the pinch, they ne'er would flinch;
 They never would fret nor whine,
Like good old bricks they stood the kicks
 In the days of Forty-Nine.

There's old " Aunt Jess," that hard old cuss,
 Who never would repent;
He never missed a single meal,
 Nor never paid a cent.
But old " Aunt Jess," like all the rest,
 At death he did resign,
And in his bloom went up the flume
 In the days of Forty-Nine.

9

There is Ragshag Jim, the roaring man,
Who could out-roar a buffalo, you bet,
He roared all day and he roared all night,
And I guess he is roaring yet.
One night Jim fell in a prospect hole,—
It was a roaring bad design,—
And in that hole Jim roared out his soul
In the days of Forty-Nine.

There is Wylie Bill, the funny man,
Who was full of funny tricks,
And when he was in a poker game
He was always hard as bricks.
He would ante you a stud, he would play you a draw,
He'd go you a hatful blind,—
In a struggle with death Bill lost his breath
In the days of Forty-Nine.

There was New York Jake, the butcher boy,
Who was fond of getting tight.
And every time he got on a spree
He was spoiling for a fight.
One night Jake rampaged against a knife
In the hands of old Bob Sine,
And over Jake they held a wake
In the days of Forty-Nine.

There was Monte Pete, I'll ne'er forget
The luck he always had,
He would deal for you both day and night

Or as long as he had a scad.
It was a pistol shot that lay Pete out,
It was his last resign,
And it caught Pete dead sure in the door
In the days of Forty-Nine.

Of all the comrades that I've had
There's none that's left to boast,
And I am left alone in my misery
Like some poor wandering ghost.
And as I pass from town to town,
They call me the rambling sign,
Since the days of old and the days of gold
And the days of Forty-Nine.

Days of Forty-Nine

You are gaz-ing now on old Tom Moore, A
rel-ic of by-gone days; 'Tis a bum-mer now they
call me,. But what cares I for praise; It is

Days of Forty-Nine—*Continued*

oft, says I, for days gone by, It's oft do I re-

pine For those days of old when we dug out the gold, In the

days of For-ty-nine, In those days of old when we

dug   out the gold,   In   the   days   of   For - ty - nine.

JOE BOWERS

MY name is Joe Bowers,
　　I've got a brother Ike,
I came here from Missouri,
Yes, all the way from Pike.
I'll tell you why I left there
And how I came to roam,
And leave my poor old mammy,
So far away from home.

I used to love a gal there,
Her name was Sallie Black,
I asked her for to marry me,
She said it was a whack.
She says to me, " Joe Bowers,
Before you hitch for life,
You ought to have a little home
To keep your little wife."

Says I, " My dearest Sallie,
O Sallie, for your sake,
I'll go to California
And try to raise a stake."
Says she to me, " Joe Bowers,
You are the chap to win,
Give me a kiss to seal the bargain,"—
And I throwed a dozen in.

Joe Bowers

I'll never forget my feelings
When I bid adieu to all.
Sal, she cotched me round the neck
And I began to bawl.
When I begun they all commenced,
You never heard the like,
How they all took on and cried
The day I left old Pike.

When I got to this here country
I hadn't nary a red,
I had such wolfish feelings
I wished myself most dead.
At last I went to mining,
Put in my biggest licks,
Came down upon the boulders
Just like a thousand bricks.

I worked both late and early
In rain and sun and snow,
But I was working for my Sallie
So 'twas all the same to Joe.
I made a very lucky strike
As the gold itself did tell,
For I was working for my Sallie,
The girl I loved so well.

But one day I got a letter
From my dear, kind brother Ike;
It came from old Missouri,
Yes, all the way from Pike.

Joe Bowers

It told me the goldarndest news
That ever you did hear,
My heart it is a-bustin'
So please excuse this tear.

I'll tell you what it was, boys,
You'll bust your sides I know;
For when I read that letter
You ought to seen poor Joe.
My knees gave 'way beneath me,
And I pulled out half my hair;
And if you ever tell this now,
You bet you'll hear me swear.

It said my Sallie was fickle,
Her love for me had fled,
That she had married a butcher,
Whose hair was awful red;
It told me more than that,
It's enough to make me swear,—
It said that Sallie had a baby
And the baby had red hair.

Now I've told you all that I can tell
About this sad affair,
'Bout Sallie marrying the butcher
And the baby had red hair.
But whether it was a boy or girl
The letter never said,
It only said its cussed hair
Was inclined to be red.

THE COWBOY'S DREAM *

L AST night as I lay on the prairie,
   And looked at the stars in the sky,
I wondered if ever a cowboy
Would drift to that sweet by and by.

   Roll on, roll on;
   Roll on, little dogies, roll on, roll on,
   Roll on, roll on;
   Roll on, little dogies, roll on.

The road to that bright, happy region
Is a dim, narrow trail, so they say;
But the broad one that leads to perdition
Is posted and blazed all the way.

They say there will be a great round-up,
And cowboys, like dogies, will stand,
To be marked by the Riders of Judgment
Who are posted and know every brand.

I know there's many a stray cowboy
Who'll be lost at the great, final sale,
When he might have gone in the green pastures
Had he known of the dim, narrow trail.

* Sung to the air of *My Bonnie Lies Over the Ocean.*

The Cowboy's Dream

I wonder if ever a cowboy
Stood ready for that Judgment Day,
And could say to the Boss of the Riders,
" I'm ready, come drive me away."

For they, like the cows that are locoed,
Stampede at the sight of a hand,
Are dragged with a rope to the round-up,
Or get marked with some crooked man's brand.

And I'm scared that I'll be a stray yearling,—
A maverick, unbranded on high,—
And get cut in the bunch with the " rusties "
When the Boss of the Riders goes by.

For they tell of another big owner
Whose ne'er overstocked, so they say,
But who always makes room for the sinner
Who drifts from the straight, narrow way.

They say he will never forget you,
That he knows every action and look;
So, for safety, you'd better get branded,
Have your name in the great Tally Book.

THE COWBOY'S LIFE *

THE bawl of a steer,
    To a cowboy's ear,
Is music of sweetest strain;
And the yelping notes
Of the gray cayotes
To him are a glad refrain.

And his jolly songs
Speed him along,
As he thinks of the little gal
With golden hair
Who is waiting there
At the bars of the home corral.

For a kingly crown
In the noisy town
His saddle he wouldn't change;
No life so free
As the life we see
Way out on the Yaso range.

His eyes are bright
And his heart as light
As the smoke of his cigarette;
There's never a care

* Attributed to James Barton Adams.

For his soul to bear,
No trouble to make him fret,

The rapid beat
Of his broncho's feet
On the sod as he speeds along,
Keeps living time
To the ringing rhyme
Of his rollicking cowboy song.

Hike it, cowboys,
For the range away
On the back of a bronc of steel,
With a careless flirt
Of the raw-hide quirt
And a dig of a roweled heel!

The winds may blow
And the thunder growl
Or the breezes may safely moan; —
A cowboy's life
Is a royal life,
His saddle his kingly throne.

Saddle up, boys,
For the work is play
When love's in the cowboy's eyes, —
When his heart is light
As the clouds of white
That swim in the summer skies.

THE KANSAS LINE

COME all you jolly cowmen, don't you want to
   go
Way up on the Kansas line?
Where you whoop up the cattle from morning till
   night
All out in the midnight rain.

   The cowboy's life is a dreadful life,
   He's driven through heat and cold;
   I'm almost froze with the water on my clothes,
   A-ridin' through heat and cold.

I've been where the lightnin', the lightnin' tangled
   in my eyes,
The cattle I could scarcely hold;
Think I heard my boss man say:
" I want all brave-hearted men who ain't afraid to
   die
To whoop up the cattle from morning till night,
Way up on the Kansas line."

Speaking of your farms and your shanty charms,
Speaking of your silver and gold,—
Take a cowman's advice, go and marry you a true
   and lovely little wife,
Never to roam, always stay at home;

22

The Kansas Line

That's a cowman's, a cowman's advice,
Way up on the Kansas line.

Think I heard the noisy cook say,
" Wake up, boys, it's near the break of day,"—
Way up on the Kansas line,
And slowly we will rise with the sleepy feeling eyes,
Way up on the Kansas line.

The cowboy's life is a dreary, dreary life,
All out in the midnight rain;
I'm almost froze with the water on my clothes,
Way up on the Kansas line.

THE COWMAN'S PRAYER

NOW, O Lord, please lend me thine ear,
The prayer of a cattleman to hear,
No doubt the prayers may seem strange,
But I want you to bless our cattle range.

Bless the round-ups year by year,
And don't forget the growing steer;
Water the lands with brooks and rills
For my cattle that roam on a thousand hills.

Prairie fires, won't you please stop?
Let thunder roll and water drop.
It frightens me to see the smoke;
Unless it's stopped, I'll go dead broke.

As you, O Lord, my herd behold,
It represents a sack of gold;
I think at least five cents a pound
Will be the price of beef the year around.

One thing more and then I'm through,—
Instead of one calf, give my cows two.
I may pray different from other men
But I've had my say, and now, Amen.

THE MINER'S SONG *

IN a rusty, worn-out cabin sat a broken-hearted
   leaser,
His singlejack was resting on his knee.
His old " buggy " in the corner told the same old
   plaintive tale,
His ore had left in all his poverty.
He lifted his old singlejack, gazed on its battered
   face,
And said: " Old boy, I know we're not to blame;
Our gold has us forsaken, some other path it's taken,
But I still believe we'll strike it just the same.

  " We'll strike it, yes, we'll strike it just the same,
    Although it's gone into some other's claim.
  My dear old boy don't mind it, we won't starve
    if we don't find it,
  And we'll drill and shoot and find it just the same.

" For forty years I've hammered steel and tried to
   make a strike,
I've burned twice the powder Custer ever saw.
I've made just coin enough to keep poorer than a
   snake.
My jack's ate all my books on mining law.

  * Printed as a fugitive ballad in *Grandon of Sierra,* by Charles
E. Winter.

25

I've worn gunny-sacks for overalls, and ' California
   socks,'
I've burned candles that would reach from here to
   Maine,
I've lived on powder, smoke, and bacon, that's no
   lie, boy, I'm not fakin',
But I still believe we'll strike it just the same.

" Last night as I lay sleeping in the midst of all my
   dream
My assay ran six ounces clear in gold,
And the silver it ran clean sixteen ounces to the
   seam,
And the poor old miner's joy could scarce be told.
I lay there, boy, I could not sleep, I had a feverish
   brow,
Got up, went back, and put in six holes more.
And then, boy, I was chokin' just to see the ground
   I'd broken;
But alas! alas! the miner's dream was o'er.

" We'll strike it, yes, we'll strike it just the same,
Although it's gone into some other's claim.
My dear old boy, don't mind it, we won't starve
   if we don't find it,
And I still believe I'll strike it just the same."

JESSE JAMES

JESSE JAMES was a lad that killed a-many a man;
    He robbed the Danville train.
But that dirty little coward that shot Mr. Howard
Has laid poor Jesse in his grave.

> Poor Jesse had a wife to mourn for his life,
> Three children, they were brave.
> But that dirty little coward that shot Mr.
>   Howard
> Has laid poor Jesse in his grave.

It was Robert Ford, that dirty little coward,
I wonder how he does feel,
For he ate of Jesse's bread and he slept in Jesse's bed,
Then laid poor Jesse in his grave.

Jesse was a man, a friend to the poor,
He never would see a man suffer pain;
And with his brother Frank he robbed the Chicago
    bank,
And stopped the Glendale train.

It was his brother Frank that robbed the Gallatin
    bank,
And carried the money from the town;
It was in this very place that they had a little race,
For they shot Captain Sheets to the ground.

They went to the crossing not very far from there,
And there they did the same;
With the agent on his knees, he delivered up the keys
To the outlaws, Frank and Jesse James.

It was on Wednesday night, the moon was shining
bright,
They robbed the Glendale train;
The people they did say, for many miles away,
It was robbed by Frank and Jesse James.

It was on Saturday night, Jesse was at home
Talking with his family brave,
Robert Ford came along like a thief in the night
And laid poor Jesse in his grave.

The people held their breath when they heard of
Jesse's death,
And wondered how he ever came to die.
It was one of the gang called little Robert Ford,
He shot poor Jesse on the sly.

Jesse went to his rest with his hand on his breast;
The devil will be upon his knee.
He was born one day in the county of Clay
And came from a solitary race.

This song was made by Billy Gashade,
As soon as the news did arrive;
He said there was no man with the law in his hand
Who could take Jesse James when alive.

Jesse James

Jes - se James was a lad that killed a - ma - ny a

man; He robbed the Dan - ville train; But that

dirt - y lit - tle cow - ard that shot Mis - ter

How-ard Has laid poor Jes-se in the grave.

REFRAIN.

Poor Jes-se had a wife to mourn for his life,

Three chil-dren, they were brave; But that

Jesse James—*Concluded*

dir - ty lit - tle cow - ard That shot Mis - ter How- ard Has laid poor Jes - se in the grave.

POOR LONESOME COWBOY

I AIN'T got no father,
  I ain't got no father,
I ain't got no father,
To buy the clothes I wear.

  I'm a poor, lonesome cowboy,
  I'm a poor, lonesome cowboy,
  I'm a poor, lonesome cowboy
  And a long ways from home.

I ain't got no mother,
I ain't got no mother,
I ain't got no mother
To mend the clothes I wear.

I ain't got no sister,
I ain't got no sister,
I ain't got no sister
To go and play with me.

I ain't got no brother,
I ain't got no brother,
I ain't got no brother
To drive the steers with me.

Poor Lonesome Cowboy

I ain't got no sweetheart,
I ain't got no sweetheart,
I ain't got no sweetheart
To sit and talk with me.

I'm a poor, lonesome cowboy,
I'm a poor, lonesome cowboy,
I'm a poor, lonesome cowboy
And a long ways from home.

BUENA VISTA BATTLEFIELD

ON Buena Vista battlefield
   A dying soldier lay,
His thoughts were on his mountain home
Some thousand miles away.
He called his comrade to his side,
For much he had to say,
In briefest words to those who were
Some thousand miles away.

" My father, comrade, you will tell
About this bloody fray;
My country's flag, you'll say to him,
Was safe with me to-day.
I make a pillow of it now
On which to lay my head,
A winding sheet you'll make of it
When I am with the dead.

" I know 'twill grieve his inmost soul
To think I never more
Will sit with him beneath the oak
That shades the cottage door;
But tell that time-worn patriot,
That, mindful of his fame,
Upon this bloody battlefield
I sullied not his name.

34

" My mother's form is with me now,
   Her will is in my ear,
   And drop by drop as flows my blood
   So flows from her the tear.
   And oh, when you shall tell to her
   The tidings of this day,
   Speak softly, comrade, softly speak
   What you may have to say.

" Speak not to her in blighting words
   The blighting news you bear,
   The cords of life might snap too soon,
   So, comrade, have a care.
   I am her only, cherished child,
   But tell her that I died
   Rejoicing that she taught me young
   To take my country's side.

" But, comrade, there's one more,
   She's gentle as a fawn;
   She lives upon the sloping hill
   That overlooks the lawn,
   The lawn where I shall never more
   Go forth with her in merry mood
   To gather wild-wood flowers.

" Tell her when death was on my brow
   And life receding fast,
   Her looks, her form was with me then,
   Were with me to the last.

35

Buena Vista Battlefield

On Buena Vista's bloody field
Tell her I dying lay,
And that I knew she thought of me
Some thousand miles away."

36

WESTWARD HO

I LOVE not Colorado
 Where the faro table grows,
And down the desperado
The rippling Bourbon flows;

Nor seek I fair Montana
Of bowie-lunging fame;
The pistol ring of fair Wyoming
I leave to nobler game.

Sweet poker-haunted Kansas
In vain allures the eye;
The Nevada rough has charms enough
Yet its blandishments I fly.

Shall Arizona woo me
Where the meek Apache bides?
Or New Mexico where natives grow
With arrow-proof insides?

Nay, 'tis where the grizzlies wander
And the lonely diggers roam,
And the grim Chinese from the squatter flees
That I'll make my humble home.

I'll chase the wild tarantula
And the fierce cayote I'll dare,

And the locust grim, I'll battle him
In his native wildwood lair.

Or I'll seek the gulch deserted
And dream of the wild Red man,
And I'll build a cot on a corner lot
And get rich as soon as I can.

A HOME ON THE RANGE

OH, give me a home where the buffalo roam,
   Where the deer and the antelope play,
Where seldom is heard a discouraging word
And the skies are not cloudy all day.

   Home, home on the range,
   Where the deer and the antelope play;
   Where seldom is heard a discouraging word
   And the skies are not cloudy all day.

Where the air is so pure, the zephyrs so free,
The breezes so balmy and light,
That I would not exchange my home on the range
For all of the cities so bright.

The red man was pressed from this part of the
      West,
He's likely no more to return
To the banks of Red River where seldom if ever
Their flickering camp-fires burn.

How often at night when the heavens are bright
With the light from the glittering stars,
Have I stood here amazed and asked as I gazed
If their glory exceeds that of ours.

A Home on the Range

Oh, I love these wild flowers in this dear land of ours,
The curlew I love to hear scream,
And I love the white rocks and the antelope flocks
That graze on the mountain-tops green.

Oh, give me a land where the bright diamond sand
Flows leisurely down the stream;
Where the graceful white swan goes gliding along
Like a maid in a heavenly dream.

Then I would not exchange my home on the range,
Where the deer and the antelope play;
Where seldom is heard a discouraging word
And the skies are not cloudy all day.

Home, home on the range,
Where the deer and the antelope play;
Where seldom is heard a discouraging word
And the skies are not cloudy all day.

Home on the Range

Oh, give me a home where the buf - fa - lo roam,

Where the deer and the an - te - lope play;.....

Where sel - dom is heard a dis - cour - ag - ing word

And the skies are not cloud - y all day.

REFRAIN

Home, home on the range, Where the deer and the antelope play;

Where sel - dom is heard a dis - cour - ag - ing word

Home on the Range—*Concluded*

And the skies are not cloud-y all day.

TEXAS RANGERS

COME, all you Texas rangers, wherever you
    may be,
I'll tell you of some troubles that happened unto me.
My name is nothing extra, so it I will not tell,—
And here's to all you rangers, I am sure I wish you
    well.

It was at the age of sixteen that I joined the jolly
    band,
We marched from San Antonio down to the Rio
    Grande.
Our captain he informed us, perhaps he thought it
    right,
" Before we reach the station, boys, you'll surely have
    to fight."

And when the bugle sounded our captain gave com-
    mand,
" To arms, to arms," he shouted, " and by your
    horses stand."
I saw the smoke ascending, it seemed to reach the
    sky;
The first thought that struck me, my time had come
    to die.

I saw the Indians coming, I heard them give the yell;
My feelings at that moment, no tongue can ever tell.

I saw the glittering lances, their arrows round me
flew,
And all my strength it left me and all my courage too.

We fought full nine hours before the strife was o'er,
The like of dead and wounded I never saw before.
And when the sun was rising and the Indians they
had fled,
We loaded up our rifles and counted up our dead.

And all of us were wounded, our noble captain slain,
And the sun was shining sadly across the bloody
plain.
Sixteen as brave rangers as ever roamed the West
Were buried by their comrades with arrows in their
breast.

'Twas then I thought of mother, who to me in tears
did say,
" To you they are all strangers, with me you had
better stay."
I thought that she was childish, the best she did not
know;
My mind was fixed on ranging and I was bound
to go.

Perhaps you have a mother, likewise a sister too,
And maybe you have a sweetheart to weep and mourn
for you;

If that be your situation, although you'd like to roam,
I'd advise you by experience, you had better stay at
    home.

I have seen the fruits of rambling, I know its hard-
    ships well;
I have crossed the Rocky Mountains, rode down the
    streets of hell;
I have been in the great Southwest where the wild
    Apaches roam,
And I tell you from experience you had better stay
    at home.

And now my song is ended; I guess I have sung
    enough;
The life of a ranger I am sure is very tough.
And here's to all you ladies, I am sure I wish you
    well,
I am bound to go a-ranging, so ladies, fare you well.

THE MORMON BISHOP'S LAMENT

I AM a Mormon bishop and I will tell you what I
know.
I joined the confraternity some forty years ago.
I then had youth upon my brow and eloquence my
tongue,
But I had the sad misfortune then to meet with
Brigham Young.

He said, " Young man, come join our band and bid
hard work farewell,
You are too smart to waste your time in toil by hill
and dell;
There is a ripening harvest and our hooks shall find
the fool
And in the distant nations we shall train them in
our school."

I listened to his preaching and I learned all the role,
And the truth of Mormon doctrines burned deep
within my soul.
I married sixteen women and I spread my new belief,
I was sent to preach the gospel to the pauper and
the thief.

'Twas in the glorious days when Brigham was our
only Lord and King,

And his wild cry of defiance from the Wasatch tops
    did ring.
'Twas when that bold Bill Hickman and that
    Porter Rockwell led,
And in the blood atonements the pits received the
    dead.

They took in Dr. Robertson and left him in his
    gore,
And the Aiken brothers sleep in peace on Nephi's
    distant shore.
We marched to Mountain Meadows and on that
    glorious field
With rifle and with hatchet we made man and
    woman yield.

'Twas there we were victorious with our legions
    fierce and brave.
We left the butchered victims on the ground without
    a grave.
We slew the load of emigrants on Sublet's lonely
    road
And plundered many a trader of his then most pre-
    cious load.

Alas for all the powers that were in the by-gone
    time.
What we did as deeds of glory are condemned as
    bloody crime.

No more the blood atonements keep the doubting
  one in fear,
While the faithful were rewarded with a wedding
  once a year.

As the nation's chieftain president says our days of
  rule are o'er
And his marshals with their warrants are on watch
  at every door,
Old John he now goes skulking on the by-roads of
  our land,
Or unknown he keeps in hiding with the faithful of
  our band.

Old Brigham now is stretched beneath the cold and
  silent clay,
And the chieftains now are fallen that were mighty
  in their day;
Of the six and twenty women that I wedded long
  ago
There are two now left to cheer me in these awful
  hours of woe.
The rest are scattered where the Gentile's flag's
  unfurled
And two score of my daughters are now numbered
  with the world.

Oh, my poor old bones are aching and my head is
  turning gray;

The Mormon Bishop's Lament

Oh, the scenes were black and awful that I've witnessed in my day.
Let my spirit seek the mansion where old Brigham's
gone to dwell,
For there's no place for Mormons but the lowest
pits of hell.

DAN TAYLOR

DAN TAYLOR is a rollicking cuss,
  A frisky son of a gun,
He loves to court the maidens
And he savies how it's done.

He used to be a cowboy
And they say he wasn't slow,
He could ride the bucking bronco
And swing the long lasso.

He could catch a maverick by the head
Or heel him on the fly,
He could pick up his front ones
.Whenever he chose to try.

He used to ride most anything;
Now he seldom will.
He says they cut some caper in the air
Of which he's got his fill.

He is done and quit the business,
Settled down to quiet life,
And he's hunting for some maiden
Who will be his little wife,—

Dan Taylor

One who will wash and patch his britches
And feed the setting hen,
Milk old Blue and Brindy,
And tend to baby Ben.

Then he'll build a cozy cottage
And furnish it complete,
He'll decorate the walls inside
With pictures new and sweet.

He will leave off riding broncos
And be a different man;
He will do his best to please his wife
In every way he can.

Then together in double harness
They will trot along down the line,
Until death shall call them over
To a bright and sunny clime.

May your joys be then completed
And your sorrows have amend,
Is the fondest wish of the writer,—
Your true and faithful friend.

WHEN WORK IS DONE THIS FALL

A GROUP of jolly cowboys, discussing plans at ease,
Says one, " I'll tell you something, boys, if you will listen, please.
I am an old cow-puncher and here I'm dressed in rags,
And I used to be a tough one and take on great big jags.

" But I've got a home, boys, a good one, you all know,
Although I have not seen it since long, long ago.
I'm going back to Dixie once more to see them all;
Yes, I'm going to see my mother when the work's all done this fall.

" After the round-ups are over and after the shipping is done,
I am going right straight home, boys, ere all my money is gone.
I have changed my ways, boys, no more will I fall;
And I am going home, boys, when work is done this fall.

" When I left home, boys, my mother for me cried,
Begged me not to go, boys, for me she would have died;

53

My mother's heart is breaking, breaking for me,
that's all,
And with God's help I'll see her when the work's all
done this fall."

That very night this cowboy went out to stand his
guard;
The night was dark and cloudy and storming very
hard;
The cattle they got frightened and rushed in wild
stampede,
The cowboy tried to head them, riding at full speed.

While riding in the darkness so loudly did he shout,
Trying his best to head them and turn the herd about,
His saddle horse did stumble and on him did fall,
The poor boy won't see his mother when the work's
all done this fall.

His body was so mangled the boys all thought him
dead,
They picked him up so gently and laid him on a bed;
He opened wide his blue eyes and looking all
around
He motioned to his comrades to sit near him on the
ground.

"Boys, send mother my wages, the wages I have
earned,
For I'm afraid, boys, my last steer I have turned.

When Work Is Done This Fall

I'm going to a new range, I hear my Master's call,
And I'll not see my mother when the work's all
done this fall.

" Fred, you take my saddle; George, you take my
bed;
Bill, you take my pistol after I am dead,
And think of me kindly when you look upon them
all,
For I'll not see my mother when work is done this
fall."

Poor Charlie was buried at sunrise, no tombstone at
his head,
Nothing but a little board and this is what it said,
" Charlie died at daybreak, he died from a fall,
And he'll not see his mother when the work's all
done this fall."

SIOUX INDIANS

I'LL sing you a song, though it may be a sad one,
  Of trials and troubles and where they first begun;
I left my dear kindred, my friends, and my home,
Across the wild deserts and mountains to roam.

I crossed the Missouri and joined a large train
Which bore us over mountain and valley and plain;
And often of evenings out hunting we'd go
To shoot the fleet antelope and wild buffalo.

We heard of Sioux Indians all out on the plains
A-killing poor drivers and burning their trains,—
A-killing poor drivers with arrows and bow,
When captured by Indians no mercy they show.

We traveled three weeks till we came to the Platte
And pitched out our tents at the end of the flat,
We spread down our blankets on the green grassy
    ground,
While our horses and mules were grazing around.

While taking refreshment we heard a low yell,
The whoop of Sioux Indians coming up from the dell;
We sprang to our rifles with a flash in each eye,
" Boys," says our brave leader, " we'll fight till we
    die."

Sioux Indians

They made a bold dash and came near to our train
And the arrows fell around us like hail and like rain,
But with our long rifles we fed them cold lead
Till many a brave warrior around us lay dead.

We shot their bold chief at the head of his band.
He died like a warrior with a gun in his hand.
When they saw their bold chief lying dead in his
    gore,
They whooped and they yelled and we saw them no
    more.

With our small band,— there were just twenty-
    four,—
And the Sioux Indians there were five hundred or
    more,—
We fought them with courage; we spoke not a word,
Till the end of the battle was all that was heard.

We hitched up our horses and we started our train;
Three more bloody battles this trip on the plain;
And in our last battle three of our brave boys fell,
And we left them to rest in a green, shady dell.

THE OLD CHISHOLM TRAIL

COME along, boys, and listen to my tale,
 I'll tell you of my troubles on the old Chis-
    holm trail.

> Coma ti yi youpy, youpy ya, youpy ya,
> Coma ti yi youpy, youpy ya.

I started up the trail October twenty-third,
I started up the trail with the 2-U herd.

Oh, a ten dollar hoss and a forty dollar saddle,—
And I'm goin' to punchin' Texas cattle.

I woke up one morning on the old Chisholm trail,
Rope in my hand and a cow by the tail.

I'm up in the mornin' afore daylight
And afore I sleep the moon shines bright.

Old Ben Bolt was a blamed good boss,
But he'd go to see the girls on a sore-backed hoss.

Old Ben Bolt was a fine old man
And you'd know there was whiskey wherever he'd
    land.

My hoss throwed me off at the creek called Mud,
My hoss throwed me off round the 2-U herd.

Last time I saw him he was going cross the level
A-kicking up his heels and a-running like the devil.

It's cloudy in the West, a-looking like rain,
And my damned old slicker's in the wagon again.

Crippled my hoss, I don't know how,
Ropin' at the horns of a 2-U cow.

We hit Caldwell and we hit her on the fly,
We bedded down the cattle on the hill close by.

No chaps, no slicker, and it's pouring down rain,
And I swear, by god, I'll never night-herd again.

Feet in the stirrups and seat in the saddle,
I hung and rattled with them long-horn cattle.

Last night I was on guard and the leader broke the
    ranks,
I hit my horse down the shoulders and I spurred him
    in the flanks.

The wind commenced to blow, and the rain began to
    fall,
Hit looked, by grab, like we was goin' to loss 'em all.

The Old Chisholm Trail

I jumped in the saddle and grabbed holt the horn,
Best blamed cow-puncher ever was born.

I popped my foot in the stirrup and gave a little yell,
The tail cattle broke and the leaders went to hell.

I don't give a damn if they never do stop;
I'll ride as long as an eight-day clock.

Foot in the stirrup and hand on the horn,
Best damned cowboy ever was born.

I herded and I hollered and I done very well,
Till the boss said, " Boys, just let 'em go to hell."

Stray in the herd and the boss said kill it,
So I shot him in the rump with the handle of the
    skillet.

We rounded 'em up and put 'em on the cars,
And that was the last of the old Two Bars.

Oh it's bacon and beans most every day,—
I'd as soon be a-eatin' prairie hay.

I'm on my best horse and I'm goin' at a run,
I'm the quickest shootin' cowboy that ever pulled a
    gun.

I went to the wagon to get my roll,
To come back to Texas, dad-burn my soul.

I went to the boss to draw my roll,
He had it figgered out I was nine dollars in the hole.

I'll sell my outfit just as soon as I can,
I won't punch cattle for no damned man.

Goin' back to town to draw my money,
Goin' back home to see my honey.

With my knees in the saddle and my seat in the sky,
I'll quit punching cows in the sweet by and by.

    Coma ti yi youpy, youpy ya, youpy ya,
    Coma ti yi youpy, youpy ya.

The Old Chisholm Trail

Come a-long, boys, and list-en to my tale, I'll

tell you of my trou-bles on the old Chisholm trail.

REFRAIN

Co-ma ti yi you-pe, you-pe ya, you-pe ya,

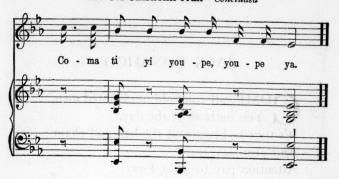

Co - ma ti yi you - pe, you - pe ya.

JACK DONAHOO

COME, all you bold, undaunted men,
  You outlaws of the day,
It's time to beware of the ball and chain
And also slavery.
Attention pay to what I say,
And verily if you do,
I will relate you the actual fate
Of bold Jack Donahoo.

He had scarcely landed, as I tell you,
Upon Australia's shore,
Than he became a real highwayman,
As he had been before.
There was Underwood and Mackerman,
And Wade and Westley too,
These were the four associates
Of bold Jack Donahoo.

Jack Donahoo, who was so brave,
Rode out that afternoon,
Knowing not that the pain of death
Would overtake him soon.
So quickly then the horse police
From Sidney came to view;
" Begone from here, you cowardly dogs,"
Says bold Jack Donahoo.

Jack Donahoo

The captain and the sergeant
Stopped then to decide.
" Do you intend to fight us
Or unto us resign? "
" To surrender to such cowardly dogs
Is more than I will do,
This day I'll fight if I lose my life,"
Says bold Jack Donahoo.

The captain and the sergeant
The men they did divide;
They fired from behind him
And also from each side;
It's six police he did shoot down
Before the fatal ball
Did pierce the heart of Donahoo
And cause bold Jack to fall.

And when he fell, he closed his eyes,
He bid the world adieu;
Come, all you boys, and sing the song
Of bold Jack Donahoo.

UTAH CARROLL

A<small>ND</small> as, my friend, you ask me what makes me
    sad and still,
And why my brow is darkened like the clouds upon
    the hill;
Run in your pony closer and I'll tell to you the tale
Of Utah Carroll, my partner, and his last ride on the
    trail.

'Mid the cactus and the thistles of Mexico's fair
    lands,
Where the cattle roam in thousands, a-many a herd
    and brand,
There is a grave with neither headstone, neither date
    nor name,—
There lies my partner sleeping in the land from which
    I came.

We rode the range together and had rode it side by
    side;
I loved him as a brother, I wept when Utah died;
We were rounding up one morning, our work was
    almost done,
When on the side the cattle started on a mad and
    fearless run.

The boss man's little daughter was holding on that
    side.

She rushed; the cattle saw the blanket, they charged
    with maddened fear.
And little Varro, seeing the danger, turned her pony
    a pace
And leaning in the saddle, tied the blanket in its
    place.

In leaning, she lost her balance and fell in front of
    that wild tide.
Utah's voice controlled the round-up. "Lay still,
    little Varro," he cried.
His only hope was to raise her, to catch her at full
    speed,
And oft-times he had been known to catch the trail
    rope off his steed.

His pony reached the maiden with a firm and steady
    bound;
Utah swung out from the saddle to catch her from
    the ground.
He swung out from the saddle, I thought her safe
    from harm,
As he swung in his saddle to raise her in his arm.

But the cinches of his saddle had not been felt before,
And his back cinch snapt asunder and he fell by the
    side of Varro.
He picked up the blanket and swung it over his head
And started across the prairie; "Lay still, little
    Varro," he said.

Well, he got the stampede turned and saved little
    Varro, his friend.
Then he turned to face the cattle and meet his fatal
    end.
His six-shooter from his pocket, from the scabbard
    he quickly drew,—
He was bound to die defended as all young cowboys
    do.

His six-shooter flashed like lightning, the report rang
    loud and clear;
As the cattle rushed in and killed him he dropped
    the leading steer.
And when we broke the circle where Utah's body lay,
With many a wound and bruise his young life ebbed
    away.

" And in some future morning," I heard the preacher
    say,
" I hope we'll all meet Utah at the round-up far
    away."
Then we wrapped him in a blanket sent by his little
    friend,
And it was that very red blanket that brought him
    to his end.

THE BULL-WHACKER

I'M a lonely bull-whacker
On the Red Cloud line,
I can lick any son of a gun
That will yoke an ox of mine.
And if I can catch him,
You bet I will or try,
I'd lick him with an ox-bow,—
Root hog or die.

It's out on the road
With a very heavy load,
With a very awkward team
And a very muddy road,
You may whip and you may holler,
But if you cuss it's on the sly;
Then whack the cattle on, boys,—
Root hog or die.

It's out on the road
These sights are to be seen,
The antelope and buffalo,
The prairie all so green,—
The antelope and buffalo,
The rabbit jumps so high;
It's whack the cattle on, boys,—
Root hog or die.

It's every day at twelve
There's something for to do;
And if there's nothing else,
There's a pony for to shoe;
I'll throw him down,
And still I'll make him lie;
Little pig, big pig,
Root hog or die.

Now perhaps you'd like to know
What we have to eat,
A little piece of bread
And a little dirty meat,
A little black coffee,
And whiskey on the sly;
It's whack the cattle on, boys,—
Root hog or die.

There's hard old times on Bitter Creek
That never can be beat,
It was root hog or die
Under every wagon sheet;
We cleaned up all the Indians,
Drank all the alkali,
And it's whack the cattle on, boys,—
Root hog or die.

There was good old times in Salt Lake
That never can pass by,
It was there I first spied
My China girl called Wi.

She could smile, she could chuckle,
She could roll her hog eye;
Then it's whack the cattle on, boys,—
Root hog or die.

Oh, I'm going home
Bull-whacking for to spurn,
I ain't got a nickel,
And I don't give a dern.
'Tis when I meet a pretty girl,
You bet I will or try,
I'll make her my little wife,—
Root hog or die.

THE "METIS" SONG OF THE BUFFALO HUNTERS

BY ROBIDEAU

HURRAH for the buffalo hunters!
　　Hurrah for the cart brigade!
That creak along on its winding way,
　　While we dance and sing and play.
Hurrah, hurrah for the cart brigade!

Hurrah for the Pembinah hunters!
　　Hurrah for its cart brigade!
For with horse and gun we roll along
　　O'er mountain and hill and plain.
Hurrah, hurrah for the cart brigade!

We whipped the Sioux and scalped them too,
　　While on the western plain,
And rode away on our homeward way
　　With none to say us nay,—
Hurrah, hurrah for the cart brigade!　Hurrah!

Mon ami, mon ami, hurrah for our black-haired
　　　girls!
　　That braved the Sioux and fought them too,
While on Montana's plains.
　　We'll hold them true and love them too,

The "Metis" Song of the Buffalo Hunters

While on the trail of the Pembinah, hurrah!
   Hurrah, hurrah for the cart brigade of Pem-
      binah!

We have the skins and the meat so sweet.
   And we'll sit by the fire in the lodge so neat,
While the wind blows cold and the snow is deep.
   Then roll in our robes and laugh as we sleep.
Hurrah, hurrah for the cart brigade!   Hurrah!
   Hurrah! Hurrah!

THE COWBOY'S LAMENT

AS I walked out in the streets of Laredo,
  As I walked out in Laredo one day,
I spied a poor cowboy wrapped up in white linen,
Wrapped up in white linen as cold as the clay.

"Oh, beat the drum slowly and play the fife lowly,
  Play the Dead March as you carry me along;
  Take me to the green valley, there lay the sod
      o'er me,
  For I'm a young cowboy and I know I've done
      wrong.

"I see by your outfit that you are a cowboy,"
These words he did say as I boldly stepped by.
"Come sit down beside me and hear my sad story;
I was shot in the breast and I know I must die.

"Let sixteen gamblers come handle my coffin,
  Let sixteen cowboys come sing me a song,
  Take me to the graveyard and lay the sod o'er me,
  For I'm a poor cowboy and I know I've done
      wrong.

"My friends and relations, they live in the Nation,
They know not where their boy has gone.
He first came to Texas and hired to a ranchman,
Oh, I'm a young cowboy and I know I've done wrong.

The Cowboy's Lament

" Go write a letter to my gray-haired mother,
And carry the same to my sister so dear;
But not a word of this shall you mention
When a crowd gathers round you my story to hear.

" Then beat your drum lowly and play your fife
slowly,
  Beat the Dead March as you carry me along;
  We all love our cowboys so young and so handsome,
  We all love our cowboys although they've done
  wrong. '

" There is another more dear than a sister,
She'll bitterly weep when she hears I am gone.
There is another who will win her affections,
For I'm a young cowboy and they say I've done
wrong.

" Go gather around you a crowd of young cowboys,
And tell them the story of this my sad fate;
Tell one and the other before they go further
To stop their wild roving before 'tis too late.

" Oh, muffle your drums, then play your fifes mer-
rily;
  Play the Dead March as you go along.
  And fire your guns right over my coffin;
  There goes an unfortunate boy to his home.

75

The Cowboy's Lament

" It was once in the saddle I used to go dashing,
It was once in the saddle I used to go gay;
First to the dram-house, then to the card-house,
Got shot in the breast, I am dying to-day.

" Get six jolly cowboys to carry my coffin;
Get six pretty maidens to bear up my pall.
Put bunches of roses all over my coffin,
Put roses to deaden the clods as they fall.

" Then swing your rope slowly and rattle your spurs
lowly,
And give a wild whoop as you carry me along;
And in the grave throw me and roll the sod o'er
me,
For I'm a young cowboy and I know I've done
wrong.

" Go bring me a cup, a cup of cold water,
To cool my parched lips," the cowboy said;
Before I turned, the spirit had left him
And gone to its Giver,— the cowboy was dead.

We beat the drum slowly and played the fife
lowly,
And bitterly wept as we bore him along;
For we all loved our comrade, so brave, young,
and handsome,
We all loved our comrade although he'd done
wrong.

LOVE IN DISGUISE

AS William and Mary stood by the seashore
Their last farewell to take,
Returning no more, little Mary she said,
" Why surely my heart will break."
" Oh, don't be dismayed, little Mary," he said,
As he pressed the dear girl to his side,
" In my absence don't mourn, for when I return
I'll make little Mary my bride."

Three years passed on without any news.
One day as she stood by the door
A beggar passed by with a patch on his eye,
" I'm home, oh, do pity, my love;
Have compassion on me, your friend I will be.
Your fortune I'll tell besides.
The lad you mourn will never return
To make little Mary his bride."

She startled and trembled and then she did say,
" All the fortune I have I freely give
If what I ask you will tell unto me,—
Say, does young William yet live? "
" He lives and is true and poverty poor,
And shipwreck has suffered beside;
He'll return no more, because he is poor,
To make little Mary his bride."

" No tongue can tell the joy I do feel
Although his misfortune I mourn,
And he's welcome to me though poverty poor,
His jacket all tattered and torn.
I love him so dear, so true and sincere,
I'll have no other beside;
Those with riches enrobed and covered with gold
Can't make little Mary their bride."

The beggar then tore the patch from his eye,
His crutches he laid by his side,
Coat, jacket and bundle; cheeks red as a rose,
'Twas William that stood by her side.
" Then excuse me, dear maid," to her he said,
" It was only your love I tried."
So he hastened away at the close of the day
To make little Mary his bride.

MUSTANG GRAY

THERE once was a noble ranger,
  They called him Mustang Gray;
He left his home when but a youth,
Went ranging far away.

  But he'll go no more a-ranging,
  The savage to affright;
  He has heard his last war-whoop,
  And fought his last fight.

He ne'er would sleep within a tent,
No comforts would he know;
But like a brave old Tex-i-an,
A-ranging he would go.

When Texas was invaded
By a mighty tyrant foe,
He mounted his noble war-horse
And a-ranging he did go.

Once he was taken prisoner,
Bound in chains upon the way,
He wore the yoke of bondage
Through the streets of Monterey.

A senorita loved him,
And followed by his side;

She opened the gates and gave to him
Her father's steed to ride.

God bless the senorita,
The belle of Monterey,
She opened wide the prison door
And let him ride away.

And when this veteran's life was spent,
It was his last command
To bury him on Texas soil
On the banks of the Rio Grande;

And there the lonely traveler,
When passing by his grave,
Will shed a farewell tear
O'er the bravest of the brave.

And he'll go no more a-ranging,
The savage to affright;
He has heard his last war-whoop,
And fought his last fight.

YOUNG COMPANIONS

COME all you young companions
    And listen unto me,
I'll tell you a story
Of some bad company.

I was born in Pennsylvania
Among the beautiful hills
And the memory of my childhood
Is warm within me still.

I did not like my fireside,
I did not like my home;
I had in view far rambling,
So far away did roam.

I had a feeble mother,
She oft would plead with me;
And the last word she gave me
Was to pray to God in need.

I had two loving sisters,
As fair as fair could be,
And oft beside me kneeling
They oft would plead with me.

I bid adieu to loved ones,
To my home I bid farewell,

And I landed in Chicago
In the very depth of hell.

It was there I took to drinking,
I sinned both night and day,
And there within my bosom
A feeble voice would say:

" Then fare you well, my loved one,
May God protect my boy,
And blessings ever with him
Throughout his manhood joy."

I courted a fair young maiden,
Her name I will not tell,
For I should ever disgrace her
Since I am doomed for hell.

It was on one beautiful evening,
The stars were shining bright,
And with a fatal dagger
I bid her spirit flight.

So justice overtook me,
You all can plainly see,
My soul is doomed forever
Throughout eternity.

It's now I'm on the scaffold,
My moments are not long;
You may forget the singer
But don't forget the song.

LACKEY BILL

COME all you good old boys and listen to my
    rhymes,
We are west of Eastern Texas and mostly men of
    crimes;
Each with a hidden secret well smothered in his breast,
Which brought us out to Mexico, way out here in
    the West.

My parents raised me tenderly, they had no child
    but me,
Till I began to ramble and with them could never
    agree.
My mind being bent on rambling did grieve their poor
    hearts sore,
To leave my aged parents them to see no more.

I was borned and raised in Texas, though never come
    to fame,
A cowboy by profession, C. W. King, by name.
Oh, when the war was ended I did not like to work,
My brothers were not happy, for I had learned to
    shirk.

In fact I was not able, my health was very bad,
I had no constitution, I was nothing but a lad.
I had no education, I would not go to school,
And living off my parents I thought it rather cool.

Lackey Bill

So I set a resolution to travel to the West,
My parents they objected, but still I thought it best.
It was out on the Seven Rivers all out on the Pecos
    stream,
It was there I saw a country I thought just suited me.

I thought I would be no stranger and lead a civil
    life,
In order to be happy would choose myself a wife.
On one Sabbath evening in the merry month of May
To a little country singing I happened there to stray.

It was there I met a damsel I never shall forget,
The impulse of that moment remains within me yet.
We soon became acquainted, I thought she would fill
    the bill,
She seemed to be good-natured, which helps to climb
    the hill.

She was a handsome figure though not so very tall;
Her hair was red as blazes, I hate it worst of all.
I saw her home one evening in the presence of her
    pap,
I bid them both good evening with a note left in her
    lap.

And when I got an answer I read it with a rush,
I found she had consented, my feelings was a hush.
But now I have changed my mind, boys, I am sure I
    wish her well.

Here's to that precious jewel, I'm sure I wish her
well.

This girl was Miss Mollie Walker who fell in love
with me,
She was a lovely Western girl, as lovely as could be,
She was so tall, so handsome, so charming and so
fair,
There is not a girl in this whole world with her I
could compare.

She said my pockets would be lined with gold, hard
work then I'd leave o'er
If I'd consent to live with her and say I'd roam no
more.
My mind began to ramble and it grieved my poor
heart sore,
To leave my darling girl, her to see no more.

I asked if it made any difference if I crossed o'er the
plains;
She said it made no difference if I returned again.
So we kissed, shook hands, and parted, I left that
girl behind.
She said she'd prove true to me till death proved her
unkind.

I rode in the town of Vagus, all in the public square;
The mail coach had arrived, the post boy met me
there.

He handed me a letter that gave me to understand
That the girl I loved in Texas had married another
man.

So I read a little farther and found those words were
true.
I turned myself all around, not knowing what to do.
I'll sell my horse, saddle, and bridle, cow-driving I'll
resign,
I'll search this world from town to town for the girl
I left behind.

Here the gold I find in plenty, the girls to me are
kind,
But my pillow is haunted with the girl I left behind.
It's trouble and disappointment is all that I can see,
For the dearest girl in all the world has gone square
back on me.

WHOOPEE TI YI YO, GIT ALONG LITTLE DOGIES

A S I walked out one morning for pleasure,
   I spied a cow-puncher all riding alone;
His hat was throwed back and his spurs was a
   jingling,
As he approached me a-singin' this song,

   Whoopee ti yi yo, git along little dogies,
   It's your misfortune, and none of my own.
   Whoopee ti yi yo, git along little dogies,
   For you know Wyoming will be your new home.

Early in the spring we round up the dogies,
Mark and brand and bob off their tails;
Round up our horses, load up the chuck-wagon,
Then throw the dogies upon the trail.

It's whooping and yelling and driving the dogies;
Oh how I wish you would go on;
It's whooping and punching and go on little
   dogies,
For you know Wyoming will be your new home.

Some boys goes up the trail for pleasure,
But that's where you get it most awfully wrong;
For you haven't any idea the trouble they give us
While we go driving them all along.

Whoopee Ti Yi Yo, Git Along Little Dogies

When the night comes on and we hold them on the
    bedground,
These little dogies that roll on so slow;
Roll up the herd and cut out the strays,
And roll the little dogies that never rolled before.

Your mother she was raised way down in Texas,
Where the jimson weed and sand-burrs grow;
Now we'll fill you up on prickly pear and cholla
Till you are ready for the trail to Idaho.

Oh, you'll be soup for Uncle Sam's Injuns;
" It's beef, heap beef," I hear them cry.
Git along, git along, git along little dogies
You're going to be beef steers by and by.

Whoopee Ti Yi Yo, Git Along Little Dogies

As I was a-walk-ing one morn-ing for pleasure,

I spied a cow-punch-er all rid-ing a-lone;

His hat was throw'd back and his spurs was a-jing-lin',

As he ap-proach'd me a - sing - in' this song:

REFRAIN.

Whoopee ti yi yo, git a - long lit - tle dog - ies,

Its your mis - for - tune and none of my own.

Whoop-ee ti yi yo, git a-long lit-tle dog-ies,

For you know Wy - o-ming will be your new home.

THE U-S-U RANGE

O COME cowboys and listen to my song,
  I'm in hopes I'll please you and not keep you
  long;
I'll sing you of things you may think strange
About West Texas and the U-S-U range.

You may go to Stamford and there see a man
Who wears a white shirt and is asking for hands;
You may ask him for work and he'll answer you
    short,
He will hurry you up, for he wants you to start.
He will put you in a wagon and be off in the rain,
You will go up on Tongue River on the U-S-U range.

You will drive up to the ranch and there you will
    stop.
It's a little sod house with dirt all on top.
You will ask what it is and they will tell you out
    plain
That it's the ranch house on the U-S-U range.

You will go in the house and he will begin to explain;
You will see some blankets rolled up on the floor;
You may ask what it is and they will tell you out
    plain
That it is the bedding on the U-S-U range.

The U-S-U Range

You are up in the morning at the daybreak
To eat cold beef and U-S-U steak,
And out to your work no matter if it's rain,—
And that is the life on the U-S-U range.

You work hard all day and come in at night,
And turn your horse loose, for they say it's all right,
And set down to supper and begin to complain
Of the chuck that you eat on the U-S-U range.

The grub that you get is beans and cold rice
And U-S-U steak cooked up very nice;
And if you don't like that you needn't complain,
For that's what you get on the U-S-U range.

Now, kind friends, I must leave you, I no longer can
    remain,
I hope I have pleased you and given you no pain.
But when I am gone, don't think me strange,
For I have been a cow-puncher on the U-S-U range.

I'M A GOOD OLD REBEL

OH, I'm a good old rebel, that's what I am;
And for this land of freedom, I don't care a
damn,
I'm glad I fought agin her, I only wish we'd won,
And I don't axe any pardon for anything I've done.

I served with old Bob Lee, three years about,
Got wounded in four places and starved at Point
Lookout;
I caught the rheumatism a-campin' in the snow,
But I killed a *chance* of Yankees and wish I'd killed
some mo'.

For I'm a good old rebel, etc.

I hate the constitooshin, this great republic too;
I hate the mouty eagle, an' the uniform so blue;
I hate their glorious banner, an' all their flags an'
fuss,
Those lyin', thievin' Yankees, I hate 'em wuss an'
wuss.

For I'm a good old rebel, etc.

I won't be re-constructed! I'm better now than
them;

I'm a Good Old Rebel

And for a carpet-bagger, I don't give a damn;
So I'm off for the frontier, soon as I can go,
I'll prepare me a weapon and start for Mexico.

For I'm a good old rebel, etc.

THE COWBOY

ALL day long on the prairies I ride,
Not even a dog to trot by my side;
My fire I kindle with chips gathered round,
My coffee I boil without being ground.

I wash in a pool and wipe on a sack;
I carry my wardrobe all on my back;
For want of an oven I cook bread in a pot,
And sleep on the ground for want of a cot.

My ceiling is the sky, my floor is the grass,
My music is the lowing of the herds as they pass;
My books are the brooks, my sermons the stones,
My parson is a wolf on his pulpit of bones.

And then if my cooking is not very complete
You can't blame me for wanting to eat.
But show me a man that sleeps more profound
Than the big puncher-boy who stretches himself on
the ground.

My books teach me ever consistence to prize,
My sermons, that small things I should not despise;
My parson remarks from his pulpit of bones
That fortune favors those who look out for their
own.

And then between me and love lies a gulf very wide.
Some lucky fellow may call her his bride.
My friends gently hint I am coming to grief,
But men must make money and women have beef.

But Cupid is always a friend to the bold,
And the best of his arrows are pointed with gold.
Society bans me so savage and dodge
That the Masons would ball me out of their lodge.

If I had hair on my chin, I might pass for the goat
That bore all the sins in the ages remote;
But why it is I can never understand,
For each of the patriarchs owned a big brand.

Abraham emigrated in search of a range,
And when water was scarce he wanted a change;
Old Isaac owned cattle in charge of Esau,
And Jacob punched cows for his father-in-law.

He started in business way down at bed rock,
And made quite a streak at handling stock;
Then David went from night-herding to using a
     sling;
And, winning the battle, he became a great king.
Then the shepherds, while herding the sheep on a
     hill,
Got a message from heaven of peace and goodwill.

The Cowboy

Music by the " Kid "

All day on the prai - rie in the sad - dle I ride,

Not e - ven a dog, boys, to trot by my side.

My fire I must kin - dle with chips gathered round,

And boil my own cof-fee with-out be-ing ground.

I wash in a pool and I wipe on a sack,

I car-ry my ward-robe all on my back.

BILL PETERS, THE STAGE DRIVER

BILL PETERS was a hustler
From Independence town;
He warn't a college scholar
Nor man of great renown,
But Bill had a way o' doing things
And doin' 'em up brown.

Bill driv the stage from Independence
Up to the Smokey Hill;
And everybody knowed him thar
As Independence Bill,—
Thar warn't no feller on the route
That driv with half the skill.

Bill driv four pair of horses,
Same as you'd drive a team,
And you'd think you was a-travelin'
On a railroad driv by steam;
And he'd git thar on time, you bet,
Or Bill 'u'd bust a seam.

He carried mail and passengers,
And he started on the dot,
And them teams o' his'n, so they say,
Was never known to trot;
But they went it in a gallop
And kept their axles hot.

When Bill's stage 'u'd bust a tire,
Or something 'u'd break down,
He'd hustle round and patch her up
And start off with a bound;
And the wheels o' that old shack o' his
Scarce ever touched the ground.

And Bill didn't low no foolin',
And when Inguns hove in sight
And bullets rattled at the stage,
He druv with all his might;
He'd holler, " Fellers, give 'em hell,
I ain't got time to fight."

Then the way them wheels 'u'd rattle,
And the way the dust 'u'd fly,
You'd think a million cattle,
Had stampeded and gone by;
But the mail 'u'd get thar just the same,
If the horses had to die.

He driv that stage for many a year
Along the Smokey Hill,
And a pile o' wild Comanches
Did Bill Peters have to kill,—
And I reckon if he'd had good luck
He'd been a drivin' still.

But he chanced one day to run agin
A bullet made o' lead,

Which was harder than he bargained for
And now poor Bill is dead;
And when they brung his body home
A barrel of tears was shed.

HARD TIMES

COME listen a while and I'll sing you a song
   Concerning the times — it will not be long —
When everybody is striving to buy,
And cheating each other, I cannot tell why,—
And it's hard, hard times.

From father to mother, from sister to brother,
From cousin to cousin, they're cheating each other.
Since cheating has grown to be so much the fashion,
I believe to my soul it will run the whole Nation,—
And it's hard, hard times.

Now there is the talker, by talking he eats,
And so does the butcher by killing his meats.
He'll toss the steelyards, and weigh it right down,
And swear it's just right if it lacks forty pounds,—
And it's hard, hard times.

And there is the merchant, as honest, we're told.
Whatever he sells you, my friend, you are sold;
Believe what I tell you, and don't be surprised
To find yourself cheated half out of your eyes,—
And it's hard, hard times.

Hard Times

And there is the lawyer you plainly will see,
He will plead your case for a very large fee,
He'll law you and tell you the wrong side is right,
And make you believe that a black horse is white,—
And it's hard, hard times.

And there is the doctor, I like to forgot,
I believe to my soul he's the worst of the lot;
He'll tell you he'll cure you for half you possess,
And when you're buried he'll take all the rest,—
And it's hard, hard times.

And there's the old bachelor, all hated with scorn,
He's like an old garment all tattered and torn,
The girls and the widows all toss him a sigh,
And think it quite right, and so do I,—
And it's hard, hard times.

And there's the young widow, coquettish and shy,
With a smile on her lips and a tear in her eye,
But when she gets married she'll cut quite a dash,
She'll give him the reins and she'll handle the cash,—
And it's hard, hard times.

And there's the young lady I like to have missed,
And I believe to my soul she'd like to be kissed;
She'll tell you she loves you with all pretence
And ask you to call again some time hence,—
And it's hard, hard times.

Hard Times

And there's the young man, the worst of the whole.
Oh, he will tell you with all of his soul,
He'll tell you he loves you and for you will die,
And when he's away he will swear it's a lie,—
And it's hard, hard times.

COLE YOUNGER

AM one of a band of highwaymen, Cole Younger
    is my name;
My crimes and depredations have brought my friends
    to shame;
The robbing of the Northfield Bank, the same I
    can't deny,
For now I am a prisoner, in the Stillwater jail I lie.

'Tis of a bold, high robbery, a story to you I'll tell,
Of a California miner who unto us befell;
We robbed him of his money and bid him go his
    way,
For which I will be sorry until my dying day.

And then we started homeward, when brother Bob
    did say:
"Now, Cole, we will buy fast horses and on them
    ride away.
We will ride to avenge our father's death and try to
    win the prize;
We will fight those anti-guerrillas until the day we
    die."

And then we rode towards Texas, that good old
    Lone Star State,
But on Nebraska's prairies the James boys we did
    meet;

With knives, guns, and revolvers we all sat down to
play,
A-drinking of good whiskey to pass the time away.

A Union Pacific railway train was the next we did
surprise,
And the crimes done by our bloody hands bring
tears into my eyes.
The engineerman and fireman killed, the conductor
escaped alive,
And now their bones lie mouldering beneath Nebraska's skies.

Then we saddled horses, northwestward we did go,
To the God-forsaken country called Min-ne-so-te-o;
I had my eye on the Northfield bank when brother
Bob did say,
"Now, Cole, if you undertake the job, you will
surely curse the day."

But I stationed out my pickets and up to the bank
did go,
And there upon the counter I struck my fatal blow.
"Just hand us over your money and make no further
delay,
We are the famous Younger brothers, we spare no
time to pray."

MISSISSIPPI GIRLS

COME, all you Mississippi girls, and listen to my
 noise,
If you happen to go West, don't you marry those
 Texian boys;
For if you do, your fortune will be
Cold jonny-cake and beefsteak, that's all that you will
 see,—
Cold jonny-cake and beefsteak, that's all that you will
 see.

When they go courting, here's what they wear:
An old leather coat, and it's all ripped and tore;
And an old brown hat with the brim tore down,
And a pair of dirty socks, they've worn the winter
 round.

When one comes in, the first thing you hear
Is, " Madam, your father has killed a deer ";
And the next thing they say when they sit down
Is, " Madam, the jonny-cake is too damned brown."

They live in a hut with hewed log wall,
But it ain't got any windows at all;
With a clap-board roof and a puncheon floor,
And that's the way all Texas o'er.

They will take you out on a live-oak hill
And there they will leave you much against your will.
They will leave you on the prairie, starve you on the
    plains,
For that is the way with the Texians,—
For that is the way with the Texians.

When they go to preaching let me tell you how they
    dress;
Just an old black shirt without any vest,
Just an old straw hat more brim than crown
And an old sock leg that they wear the winter
    round,—
And an old sock leg that they wear the winter
    round.

For your wedding supper, there'll be beef and corn-
    bread;
There it is to eat when the ceremony's said.
And when you go to milk you'll milk into a gourd;
And set it in the corner and cover it with a board;
Some gets little and some gets none,
For that is the way with the Texians,—
For that is the way with the Texians.

THE OLD MAN UNDER THE HILL

THERE was an old man who lived under the hill,
Chir-u-ra-wee, lived under the hill,
And if he ain't dead he's living there still,
Chir-u-ra-wee, living there still.

One day the old man went out to plow,
Chir-u-ra-wee, went out to plow;
'Tis good-bye the old fellow, and how are you now,
Sing chir-u-ra-wee, and how are you now.

And then another came to his house,
Chir-u-ra-wee, came to his house;
"There's one of your family I've got to have now,
Sing chir-u-ra-wee, got to have now.

"It's neither you nor your oldest son,
Chir-u-ra-wee, nor your oldest son."
"Then take my old woman and take her for fun,
Sing chir-u-ra-wee, take her for fun."

He takened her all upon his back,
Chir-u-ra-wee, upon his back,
And like an old rascal went rickity rack,
Sing chir-u-ra-wee, went rickity rack.

But when he got half way up the road,
Chir-u-ra-wee, up the road,

Says he, "You old lady, you're sure a load,"
Sing chir-u-ra-wee, you're sure a load.

He set her down on a stump to rest,
Chir-u-ra-wee, stump to rest;
She up with a stick and hit him her best.
Sing chir-u-ra-wee, hit him her best.

He taken her on to hell's old gate,
Chir-u-ra-wee, hell's old gate,
But when he got there he got there too late,
Sing chir-u-ra-wee, got there too late.

And so he had to keep his wife,
Chir-u-ra-wee, had to keep his wife,
And keep her he did for the rest of his life,
Sing chir-u-ra-wee, for the rest of his life.

JERRY, GO ILE THAT CAR

COME all ye railroad section men an' listen to
      my song,
It is of Larry O'Sullivan who now is dead and gone.
For twenty years a section boss, he niver hired a
      tar —
Oh, it's " j'int ahead and cinter back,
An' Jerry, go ile that car! "

    For twenty years a section boss, he niver hired a tar,
    But it's " j'int ahead an cinter back,
    An' Jerry, go ile that car-r-r! "

For twenty years a section boss, he worked upon the
      track,
And be it to his cred-i-it he niver had a wrack.
For he kept every j'int right up to the p'int wid the
      tap of the tampin-bar-r-r;
And while the byes was a-swimmin' up the ties,
It's " Jerry, wud yez ile that car-r-r! "

God rest ye, Larry O'Sullivan, to me ye were kind
      and good;
Ye always made the section men go out and chop me
      wood;
An' fetch me wather from the well an' chop me
      kindlin' fine;

'And any man that wouldn't lind a hand, 'twas Larry
  give him his Time.

And ivery Sunday morni-i-ing unto the gang he'd say:
" Me byes, prepare — yez be aware the ould lady
  goes to church the day.
Now, I want ivery man to pump the best he can, for
  the distance it is far-r-r;
An' we have to get in ahead of number tin —
So, Jerry, go an' ile that car-r-r! "

'Twas in November in the winter time and the
  ground all covered wid snow,
" Come put the hand-car-r-r on the track an' over
  the section go! "
Wid his big soger coat buttoned up to his t'roat, all
  weathers he would dare —
An' it's " Paddy Mack, will yez walk the track,
An' Jerry, go an' ile that car-r-r! "

" Give my respects to the roadmas-ther," poor Larry
  he did cry,
" An lave me up that I may see the ould hand-car
  before I die.
Come, j'int ahead an' cinter back,
An' Jerry, go an' ile that car-r-r! "

Then lay the spike maul upon his chist, the gauge,
  and the ould claw-bar-r-r,
  And while the byes do be fillin' up his grave,
" Oh, Jerry, go an' ile that car-r-r! "

JOHN GARNER'S TRAIL HERD

COME all you old timers and listen to my song;
  I'll make it short as possible and I'll not keep
      you long;
I'll relate to you about the time you all remember
    well
When we, with old Joe Garner, drove a beef herd
    up the trail.

When we left the ranch it was early in the spring,
We had as good a corporal as ever rope did swing,
Good hands and good horses, good outfit through
    and through,—
We went well equipped, we were a jolly crew.

We had no little herd — two thousand head or
    more —
And some as wild a brush beeves as you ever saw be-
    fore.
We swung to them all the way and sometimes by the
    tail,—
Oh, you know we had a circus as we all went up the
    trail.

All things went on well till we reached the open
    ground,
And then them cattle turned in and they gave us
    merry hell.

114

They stampeded every night that came and did it
    without fail,—
Oh, you know we had a circus as we all went up the
    trail.

We would round them up at morning and the boss
    would make a count,
And say, " Look here, old punchers, we are out quite
    an amount;
You must make all losses good and do it without
    fail
Or you will never get another job of driving up the
    trail."

When we reached Red River we gave the Inspector
    the dodge.
He swore by God Almighty, in jail old John should
    lodge.
We told him if he'd taken our boss and had him
    locked in jail,
We would shore get his scalp as we all came down
    the trail.

When we reached the Reservation, how squirmish
    we did feel,
Although we had tried old Garner and knew him
    true as steel.
And if we would follow him and do as he said do,
That old bald-headed cow-thief would surely take
    us through.

When we reached Dodge City we drew our four
months' pay.
Times was better then, boys, that was a better day.
The way we drank and gambled and threw the girls
around,—
" Say, a crowd of Texas cowboys has come to take
our town."

The cowboy sees many hardships although he takes
them well;
The fun we had upon that trip, no human tongue
can tell.
The cowboy's life is a dreary life, though his mind
it is no load,
And he always spends his money like he found it in
the road.

If ever you meet old Garner, you must meet him on
the square,
For he is the biggest cow-thief that ever tramped out
there.
But if you want to hear him roar and spin a lively
tale,
Just ask him about the time we all went up the trail.

THE OLD SCOUT'S LAMENT

COME all of you, my brother scouts,
    And join me in my song;
Come, let us sing together
Though the shadows fall so long.

Of all the old frontiersmen
That used to scour the plain,
There are but very few of them
That with us yet remain.

Day after day they're dropping off,
They're going one by one;
Our clan is fast decreasing,
Our race is almost run.

There were many of our number
That never wore the blue,
But, faithfully, they did their part,
As brave men, tried and true.

They never joined the army,
But had other work to do
In piloting the coming folks,
To help them safely through.

But, brothers, we are falling,
Our race is almost run;

The days of elk and buffalo
And beaver traps are gone.

Oh, the days of elk and buffalo!
It fills my heart with pain
To know these days are past and gone
To never come again.

We fought the red-skin rascals
Over valley, hill, and plain;
We fought him in the mountain top,
And fought him down again.

These fighting days are over;
The Indian yell resounds
No more along the border;
Peace sends far sweeter sounds.

But we found great joy, old comrades,
To hear, and make it die;
We won bright homes for gentle ones,
And now, our West, good-bye.

THE LONE BUFFALO HUNTER

IT'S of those Texas cowboys, a story I'll tell;
No name I will mention though in Texas they
do dwell.
Go find them where you will, they are all so very
brave,
And when in good society they seldom misbehave.

When the fall work is all over in the line-camp they'll
be found,
For they have to ride those lonesome lines the long
winter round;
They prove loyal to a comrade, no matter what's to
do;
And when in love with a fair one they seldom prove
untrue.

But springtime comes at last and finds them glad and
gay;
They ride out to the round-up about the first of May;
About the first of August they start up the trail,
They have to stay with the cattle, no matter rain or
hail.

But when they get to the shipping point, then they
receive their tens,
Straightway to the bar-room and gently blow them
in;

It's the height of their ambition, so I've been truly
  told,
To ride good horses and saddles and spend the silver and gold.

Those last two things I've mentioned, it is their
  heart's desire,
And when they leave the shipping point, their eyes
  are like balls of fire.
It's of those fighting cattle, they seem to have no
  fear,
A-riding bucking broncos oft is their heart's desire.

They will ride into the branding pen, a rope within
  their hands,
They will catch them by each forefoot and bring
  them to the sands;
It's altogether in practice with a little bit of sleight,
A-roping Texas cattle, it is their heart's delight.

But now comes the rising generation to take the cowboy's place,
Likewise the corn-fed granger, with his bold and
  cheeky face;
It's on those plains of Texas a lone buffalo hunter
  does stand
To tell the fate of the cowboy that rode at his right
  hand.

THE CROOKED TRAIL TO HOLBROOK

COME all you jolly cowboys that follow the
bronco steer,
I'll sing to you a verse or two your spirits for to
cheer;
It's all about a trip, a trip that I did undergo
On that crooked trail to Holbrook, in Arizona oh.

It's on the seventeenth of February, our herd it
started out,
It would have made your hearts shudder to hear
them bawl and shout,
As wild as any buffalo that ever rode the Platte,
Those dogies we were driving, and every one was
fat.

We crossed the Mescal Mountains on the way to
Gilson Flats,
And when we got to Gilson Flats, Lord, how the
wind did blow;
It blew so hard, it blew so fierce, we knew not
where to go,
But our spirits never failed us as onward we did
go,—
On that crooked trail to Holbrook, in Arizona oh.

That night we had a stampede; Christ, how the
cattle run!

We made it to our horses; I tell you, we had no fun;
Over the prickly pear and catclaw brush we quickly
made our way;
We thought of our long journey and the girls we'd
left one day.

It's long by Sombserva we slowly punched along,
While each and every puncher would sing a hearty
song
To cheer up his comrade as onward we did go,
On that crooked trail to Holbrook, in Arizona oh.

We crossed the Mongollen Mountains where the tall
pines do grow,
Grass grows in abundance, and rippling streams do
flow;
Our packs were always turning, of course our gait
was slow,
On that crooked trail to Holbrook, in Arizona oh.

At last we got to Holbrook, a little gale did blow;
It blew up sand and pebble stones and it didn't blow
them slow.
We had to drink the water from that muddy little
stream
And swallowed a peck of dirt when we tried to eat
a bean.

But the cattle now are shipped and homeward we
are bound

With a lot of as tired horses as ever could be found;
Across the reservation no danger did we fear,
But thought of wives and sweethearts and the ones
    we love so dear.
Now we are back in Globe City, our friendship there
    to share;
Here's luck to every puncher that follows the bronco
    steer.

ONLY A COWBOY

A WAY out in old Texas, that great lone star
state,
Where the mocking bird whistles both early and late;
It was in Western Texas on the old N A range
The boy fell a victim on the old staked plains.

He was only a cowboy gone on before,
He was only a cowboy, we will never see more;
He was doing his duty on the old N A range
But now he is sleeping on the old staked plains.

His crew they were numbered twenty-seven or eight,
The boys were like brothers, their friendship was
great,
When "O God, have mercy" was heard from be-
hind,—
The cattle were left to drift on the line.

He leaves a dear wife and little ones, too,
To earn them a living, as fathers oft do;
For while he was working for the loved ones so dear
He was took without warning or one word of cheer.

And while he is sleeping where the sun always shines,
The boys they go dashing along on the line;
The look on their faces it speaks to us all
Of one who departed to the home of the soul.

Only a Cowboy

He was only a cowboy gone on before,
He was only a cowboy, we will never see more;
He was doing his duty on the old N A range
But now he is sleeping on the old staked plains.

FULLER AND WARREN

YE sons of Columbia, your attention I do crave,
 While a sorrowful story I do tell,
Which happened of late, in the Indiana state,
And a hero not many could excel;
Like Samson he courted, made choice of the fair,
And intended to make her his wife;
But she, like Delilah, his heart did ensnare,
Which cost him his honor and his life.

A gold ring he gave her in token of his love,
On the face was the image of the dove;
They mutually agreed to get married with speed
And were promised by the powers above.
But the fickle-minded maiden vowed again to wed
To young Warren who lived in that place;
It was a fatal blow that caused his overthrow
And added to her shame and disgrace.

When Fuller came to hear he was deprived of his
  dear
Whom he vowed by the powers to wed,
With his heart full of woe unto Warren he did go,
And smilingly unto him he said:
" Young man, you have injured me to gratify your
  cause
By reporting that I left a prudent wife;

Acknowledge now that you have wronged me, for
      although I break the laws,
Young Warren, I'll deprive you of your life."

Then Warren, he replied: "Your request must be
      denied,
For your darling to my heart she is bound;
And further I can say that this is our wedding day,
In spite of all the heroes in town."
Then Fuller in the passion of his love and anger
      bound,—
Alas! it caused many to cry,—
At one fatal shot killed Warren on the spot,
And smilingly said, " I'm ready now to die."

The time was drawing nigh when Fuller had to die;
He bid the audience adieu.
Like an angel he did stand, for he was a handsome
      man,
On his breast he had a ribbon of blue.
Ten thousand spectators did smite him on the breast,
And the guards dropped a tear from the eye,
Saying, " Cursed be she who caused this misery,
Would to God in his stead she had to die."

The gentle god of Love looked with anger from
      above
And the rope flew asunder like the sand.
Two doctors for the pay they murdered him, they
      say,

They hung him by main strength of hand.
But the corpse it was buried and the doctors lost
    their prey,
Oh, that harlot was bribed, I do believe;
Bad women to a certainty are the downfall of men,
As Adam was beguiled by Eve.

Fuller and Warren

Ye sons of Co - lum - bia, your at - ten - tion I do crave,

While a sor - ri - ful sto - ry I do tell,

Which hap - pened of late in the In - di - an - a state,

And a he - ro... not ma -ny could ex - cel.

Like Sam - son he court - ed, made choice of the fair,

And in - tend - ed... to make her his wife;

But she, like De-li-la,... his heart did en-snare,

Which cost him his hon-or and his life.

THE TRAIL TO MEXICO

I MADE up my mind to change my way
  And quit my crowd that was so gay,
To leave my native home for a while
And to travel west for many a mile.

Whoo-a-whoo-a-whoo-a-whoo.

'Twas all in the merry month of May
When I started for Texas far away,
I left my darling girl behind,—
She said her heart was only mine.

Whoo-a-whoo-a-whoo-a-whoo.

Oh, it was when I embraced her in my arms
I thought she had ten thousand charms;
Her caresses were soft, her kisses were sweet,
Saying, " We will get married next time we meet."

Whoo-a-whoo-a-whoo-a-whoo.

It was in the year of eighty-three
That A. J. Stinson hired me.
He says, " Young fellow, I want you to go
And drive this herd to Mexico."

Whoo-a-whoo-a-whoo-a-whoo.

The Trail to Mexico

The first horse they gave me was an old black
With two big set-fasts on his back;
I padded him with gunny-sacks and my bedding all;
He went up, then down, and I got a fall.

Whoo-a-whoo-a-whoo-a-whoo.

The next they gave me was an old gray,
I'll remember him till my dying day.
And if I had to swear to the fact,
I believe he was worse off than the black.

Whoo-a-whoo-a-whoo-a-whoo.

Oh, it was early in the year
When I went on trail to drive the steer.
I stood my guard through sleet and snow
While on the trail to Mexico.

Whoo-a-whoo-a-whoo-a-whoo.

Oh, it was a long and lonesome go
As our herd rolled on to Mexico;
With laughter light and the cowboy's song
To Mexico we rolled along.

Whoo-a-whoo-a-whoo-a-whoo.

When I arrived in Mexico
I wanted to see my love but could not go;

So I wrote a letter, a letter to my dear,
But not a word from her could I hear.

Whoo-a-whoo-a-whoo-a-whoo.

When I arrived at the once loved home
I called for the darling of my own;
They said she had married a richer life,
Therefore, wild cowboy, seek another wife.

Whoo-a-whoo-a-whoo-a-whoo.

Oh, the girl she is married I do adore,
And I cannot stay at home any more;
I'll cut my way to a foreign land
Or I'll go back west to my cowboy band.

Whoo-a-whoo-a-whoo-a-whoo.

I'll go back to the Western land,
I'll hunt up my old cowboy band,—
Where the girls are few and the boys are true
And a false-hearted love I never knew.

Whoo-a-whoo-a-whoo-a-whoo.

" O Buddie, O Buddie, please stay at home,
Don't be forever on the roam.
There is many a girl more true than I,
So pray don't go where the bullets fly."

Whoo-a-whoo-a-whoo-a-whoo.

" It's curse your gold and your silver too,
God pity a girl that won't prove true;
I'll travel West where the bullets fly,
I'll stay on the trail till the day I die."

Whoo-a-whoo-a-whoo-a-whoo.

THE HORSE WRANGLER

I THOUGHT one spring just for fun
  I'd see how cow-punching was done,
And when the round-ups had begun
I tackled the cattle-king.
Says he, " My foreman is in town,
He's at the plaza, and his name is Brown,
If you'll see him, he'll take you down."
Says I, " That's just the thing."

We started for the ranch next day;
Brown augured me most all the way.
He said that cow-punching was nothing but play,
That it was no work at all,—
That all you had to do was ride,
And only drifting with the tide;
The son of a gun, oh, how he lied.
Don't you think he had his gall?

He put me in charge of a cavyard,
And told me not to work too hard,
That all I had to do was guard
The horses from getting away;
I had one hundred and sixty head,
I sometimes wished that I was dead;
When one got away, Brown's head turned red,
And there was the devil to pay.

Sometimes one would make a break,
Across the prairie he would take,
As if running for a stake,—
It seemed to them but play;
Sometimes I could not head them at all,
Sometimes my horse would catch a fall
And I'd shoot on like a cannon ball
Till the earth came in my way.

They saddled me up an old gray hack
With two set-fasts on his back,
They padded him down with a gunny sack
And used my bedding all.
When I got on he quit the ground,
Went up in the air and turned around,
And I came down and busted the ground,—
I got one hell of a fall.

They took me up and carried me in
And rubbed me down with an old stake pin.
" That's the way they all begin;
You're doing well," says Brown.
" And in the morning, if you don't die,
I'll give you another horse to try."
" Oh say, can't I walk? " says I.
Says he, " Yes, back to town."

I've traveled up and I've traveled down,
I've traveled this country round and round,
I've lived in city and I've lived in town,

But I've got this much to say:
Before you try cow-punching, kiss your wife,
Take a heavy insurance on your life,
Then cut your throat with a barlow knife,—
For it's easier done that way.

CALIFORNIA JOE

WELL, mates, I don't like stories;
    Or am I going to act
A part around the campfire
That ain't a truthful fact?
So fill your pipes and listen,
I'll tell you — let me see —
I think it was in fifty,
From that till sixty-three.

You've all heard tell of Bridger;
I used to run with Jim,
And many a hard day's scouting
I've done longside of him.
Well, once near old Fort Reno,
A trapper used to dwell;
We called him old Pap Reynolds,
The scouts all knew him well.

One night in the spring of fifty
We camped on Powder River,
And killed a calf of buffalo
And cooked a slice of liver.
While eating, quite contented,
I heard three shots or four;
Put out the fire and listened,—
We heard a dozen more.

We knew that old man Reynolds
Had moved his traps up here;
So picking up our rifles
And fixing on our gear
We moved as quick as lightning,
To save was our desire.
Too late, the painted heathens
Had set the house on fire.

We hitched our horses quickly
And waded up the stream;
While down close beside the waters
I heard a muffled scream.
And there among the bushes
A little girl did lie.
I picked her up and whispered,
" I'll save you or I'll die."

Lord, what a ride! Old Bridger
Had covered my retreat;
Sometimes that child would whisper
In voice low and sweet,
" Poor Papa, God will take him
To Mama up above;
There is no one left to love me,
There is no one left to love."

The little one was thirteen
And I was twenty-two;
I says, " I'll be your father

And love you just as true."
She nestled to my bosom,
Her hazel eyes so bright,
Looked up and made me happy,—
The close pursuit that night.

One month had passed and Maggie,
We called her Hazel Eye,
In truth was going to leave me,
Was going to say good-bye.
Her uncle, Mad Jack Reynolds,
Reported long since dead,
Had come to claim my angel,
His brother's child, he said.

What could I say? We parted,
Mad Jack was growing old;
I handed him a bank note
And all I had in gold.
They rode away at sunrise,
I went a mile or two,
And parting says, "We will meet again;
May God watch over you."

By a laughing, dancing brook
A little cabin stood,
And weary with a long day's scout,
I spied it in the wood.
The pretty valley stretched beyond,
The mountains towered above,

And near its willow banks I heard
The cooing of a dove.

'Twas one grand pleasure;
The brook was plainly seen,
Like a long thread of silver
In a cloth of lovely green;
The laughter of the water,
The cooing of the dove,
Was like some painted picture,
Some well-told tale of love.

While drinking in the country
And resting in the saddle,
I heard a gentle rippling
Like the dipping of a paddle,
And turning to the water,
A strange sight met my view,—
A lady with her rifle
In a little bark canoe.

She stood up in the center,
With her rifle to her eye;
I thought just for a second
My time had come to die.
I doffed my hat and told her,
If it was just the same,
To drop her little shooter,
For I was not her game.

She dropped the deadly weapon
And leaped from the canoe.
Says she, " I beg your pardon;
I thought you was a Sioux.
Your long hair and your buckskin
Looked warrior-like and rough;
My bead was spoiled by sunshine,
Or I'd have killed you sure enough."

" Perhaps it would've been better
If you'd dropped me then," says I;
" For surely such an angel
Would bear me to the sky."
She blushingly dropped her eyelids,
Her cheeks were crimson red;
One half-shy glance she gave me
And then hung down her head.

I took her little hand in mine;
She wondered what it meant,
And yet she drew it not away,
But rather seemed content.
We sat upon the mossy bank,
Her eyes began to fill;
The brook was rippling at our feet,
The dove was cooing still.

'Tis strong arms were thrown around her.
" I'll save you or I'll die."
I clasped her to my bosom,

143

My long lost Hazel Eye.
The rapture of that moment
Was almost heaven to me;
I kissed her 'mid the tear-drops,
Her merriment and glee.

Her heart near mine was beating
When sobbingly she said,
" My dear, my brave preserver,
They told me you were dead.
But oh, those parting words, Joe,
Have never left my mind,
You said, ' We'll meet again, Mag,'
Then rode off like the wind.

" And oh, how I have prayed, Joe,
For you who saved my life,
That God would send an angel
To guide you through all strife.
The one who claimed me from you,
My Uncle, good and true,
Is sick in yonder cabin;
Has talked so much of you.

" ' If Joe were living darling,'
He said to me last night,
' He would care for you, Maggie,
When God puts out my light.' "
We found the old man sleeping.
" Hush, Maggie, let him rest."

California Joe

The sun was slowly setting
In the far-off, glowing West.

And though we talked in whispers
He opened wide his eyes:
" A dream, a dream," he murmured,
" Alas, a dream of lies."
She drifted like a shadow
To where the old man lay.
" You had a dream, dear Uncle,
Another dream to-day?"

" Oh yes, I saw an angel
As pure as mountain snow,
And near her at my bedside
Stood California Joe."
" I'm sure I'm not an angel,
Dear Uncle, that you know;
These hands that hold your hand, too,
My face is not like snow.

" Now listen while I tell you,
For I have news to cheer;
Hazel Eye is happy,
For Joe is truly here."
It was but a few days after
The old man said to me,
" Joe, boy, she is an angel,
And good as angels be.

" For three long months she hunted,
And trapped and nursed me too;
God bless you, boy, I believe it,
She's safe along with you."
The sun was slowly sinking,
When Maggie, my wife, and I
Went riding through the valley,
The tear-drops in her eye.

" One year ago to-day, Joe,
I saw the mossy grave;
We laid him neath the daisies,
My Uncle, good and brave."
And comrade, every springtime
Is sure to find me there;
There is something in the valley
That is always fresh and fair.

Our love is always kindled
While sitting by the stream,
Where two hearts were united
In love's sweet happy dream.

THE BOSTON BURGLAR

I WAS born in Boston City, a city you all know
    well,
Brought up by honest parents, the truth to you I'll
    tell,
Brought up by honest parents and raised most ten-
    derly,
Till I became a roving man at the age of twenty-
    three.

My character was taken then, and I was sent to jail.
My friends they found it was in vain to get me out
    on bail.
The jury found me guilty, the clerk he wrote it down,
The judge he passed me sentence and I was sent to
    Charleston town.

You ought to have seen my aged father a-pleading at
    the bar,
Also my dear old mother a-tearing of her hair,
Tearing of her old gray locks as the tears came roll-
    ing down,
Saying, "Son, dear son, what have you done, that
    you are sent to Charleston town?"

They put me aboard an eastbound train one cold
    December day,

And every station that we passed, I'd hear the people
    say,
" There goes a noted burglar, in strong chains he'll
    be bound,—
For the doing of some crime or other he is sent to
    Charleston town."

There is a girl in Boston, she is a girl that I love well,
And if I ever gain my liberty, along with her I'll
    dwell;
And when I regain my liberty, bad company I will
    shun,
Night-walking, gambling, and also drinking rum.

Now, you who have your liberty, pray keep it if you
    can,
And don't go around the streets at night to break the
    laws of man;
For if you do you'll surely rue and find yourself like
    me,
A-serving out my twenty-one years in the penitentiary.

SAM BASS

SAM BASS was born in Indiana, it was his
    native home,
And at the age of seventeen young Sam began to
    roam.
Sam first came out to Texas a cowboy for to be,—
A kinder-hearted fellow you seldom ever see.

Sam used to deal in race stock, one called the
    Denton mare,
He matched her in scrub races, and took her to the
    Fair.
Sam used to coin the money and spent it just as free,
He always drank good whiskey wherever he might be.

Sam left the Collin's ranch in the merry month of
    May
With a herd of Texas cattle the Black Hills for to
    see,
Sold out in Custer City and then got on a spree,—
A harder set of cowboys you seldom ever see.

On their way back to Texas they robbed the U. P.
    train,
And then split up in couples and started out again.
Joe Collins and his partner were overtaken soon,
With all their hard-earned money they had to meet
    their doom.

Sam made it back to Texas all right side up with
    care;
Rode into the town of Denton with all his friends to
    share.
Sam's life was short in Texas; three robberies did
    he do,
He robbed all the passenger, mail, and express cars
    too.

Sam had four companions — four bold and daring
    lads —
They were Richardson, Jackson, Joe Collins, and Old
    Dad;
Four more bold and daring cowboys the rangers
    never knew,
They whipped the Texas rangers and ran the boys in
    blue.

Sam had another companion, called Arkansas for
    short,
Was shot by a Texas ranger by the name of Thomas
    Floyd;
Oh, Tom is a big six-footer and thinks he's mighty
    fly,
But I can tell you his racket,— he's a deadbeat on
    the sly.

Jim Murphy was arrested, and then released on
    bail;

He jumped his bond at Tyler and then took the train
    for Terrell;
But Mayor Jones had posted Jim and that was all a
    stall,
'Twas only a plan to capture Sam before the coming
    fall.

Sam met his fate at Round Rock, July the twenty-
    first,
They pierced poor Sam with rifle balls and emptied
    out his purse.
Poor Sam he is a corpse and six foot under clay,
And Jackson's in the bushes trying to get away.

Jim had borrowed Sam's good gold and didn't want
    to pay,
The only shot he saw was to give poor Sam away.
He sold out Sam and Barnes and left their friends to
    mourn,—
Oh, what a scorching Jim will get when Gabriel
    blows his horn.

And so he sold out Sam and Barnes and left their
    friends to mourn,
Oh, what a scorching Jim will get when Gabriel
    blows his horn.
Perhaps he's got to heaven, there's none of us can
    say,
But if I'm right in my surmise he's gone the other
    way.

Sam Bass

Sam Bass was born in In - di - an - a, It was his na - tive home; And at the age of sev - en - teen, Young Sam be - gan to roam. 'Sam

first came out to Tex-as, A cow-boy for to be; A

kind-er-heart-ed fel-low You sel-dom ev-er see.

THE ZEBRA DUN

WE were camped on the plains at the head of
the Cimarron
When along came a stranger and stopped to arger
some.
He looked so very foolish that we began to look
around,
We thought he was a greenhorn that had just 'scaped
from town.

We asked if he had been to breakfast; he hadn't had
a smear,
So we opened up the chuck-box and bade him have
his share.
He took a cup of coffee and some biscuits and some
beans,
And then began to talk and tell about foreign kings
and queens,—

About the Spanish war and fighting on the seas
With guns as big as steers and ramrods big as
trees,—
And about old Paul Jones, a mean, fighting son of a
gun,
Who was the grittiest cuss that ever pulled a gun.

Such an educated feller his thoughts just came in
herds,

He astonished all them cowboys with them jaw-
breaking words.
He just kept on talking till he made the boys all sick,
And they began to look around just how to play a
trick.

He said he had lost his job upon the Santa Fé
And was going across the plains to strike the 7-D.
He didn't say how come it, some trouble with the
boss,
But said he'd like to borrow a nice fat saddle hoss.

This tickled all the boys to death, they laughed way
down in their sleeves,—
"We will lend you a horse just as fresh and fat as
you please."
Shorty grabbed a lariat and roped the Zebra Dun
And turned him over to the stranger and waited for
the fun.

Old Dunny was a rocky outlaw that had grown so
awful wild
That he could paw the white out of the moon every
jump for a mile.
Old Dunny stood right still,— as if he didn't
know,—
Until he was saddled and ready for to go.

When the stranger hit the saddle, old Dunny quit
the earth

And traveled right straight up for all that he was
　　worth.
A-pitching and a-squealing, a-having wall-eyed fits,
His hind feet perpendicular, his front ones in the
　　bits.

We could see the tops of the mountains under Dunny
　　every jump,
But the stranger he was growed there just like the
　　camel's hump;
The stranger sat upon him and curled his black
　　mustache
Just like a summer boarder waiting for his hash.

He thumped him in the shoulders and spurred him
　　when he whirled,
To show them flunky punchers that he was the wolf
　　of the world.
When the stranger had dismounted once more upon
　　the ground,
We knew he was a thoroughbred and not a gent
　　from town;

The boss who was standing round watching of the
　　show,
Walked right up to the stranger and told him he
　　needn't go,—
" If you can use the lasso like you rode old Zebra
　　Dun,

You are the man I've been looking for ever since the
    year one."

Oh, he could twirl the lariat and he didn't do it slow,
He could catch them fore feet nine out of ten for any
    kind of dough.
And when the herd stampeded he was always on the
    spot
And set them to nothing, like the boiling of a pot.

There's one thing and a shore thing I've learned
    since I've been born,
That every educated feller ain't a plumb greenhorn.

THE BUFFALO SKINNERS

COME all you jolly fellows and listen to my
     song,
There are not many verses, it will not detain you
     long;
It's concerning some young fellows who did agree
     to go
And spend one summer pleasantly on the range of the
     buffalo.

It happened in Jacksboro in the spring of seventy-
     three,
A man by the name of Crego came stepping up to
     me,
Saying, "How do you do, young fellow, and how
     would you like to go
And spend one summer pleasantly on the range of
     the buffalo?"

"It's me being out of employment," this to Crego
     I did say,
"This going out on the buffalo range depends upon
     the pay.
But if you will pay good wages and transportation
     too,
I think, sir, I will go with you to the range of the
     buffalo."

"Yes, I will pay good wages, give transportation too,
Provided you will go with me and stay the summer through;
But if you should grow homesick, come back to Jacksboro,
I won't pay transportation from the range of the buffalo."

It's now our outfit was complete — seven able-bodied men,
With navy six and needle gun — our troubles did begin;
Our way it was a pleasant one, the route we had to go,
Until we crossed Pease River on the range of the buffalo.

It's now we've crossed Pease River, our troubles have begun.
The first damned tail I went to rip, Christ! how I cut my thumb!
While skinning the damned old stinkers our lives wasn't a show,
For the Indians watched to pick us off while skinning the buffalo.

He fed us on such sorry chuck I wished myself most dead,
It was old jerked beef, croton coffee, and sour bread.

Pease River's as salty as hell fire, the water I could
    never go,—
O God! I wished I had never come to the range of
    the buffalo.

Our meat it was buffalo hump and iron wedge bread,
And all we had to sleep on was a buffalo robe for a
    bed;
The fleas and gray-backs worked on us, O boys, it
    was not slow,
I'll tell you there's no worse hell on earth than the
    range of the buffalo.

Our hearts were cased with buffalo hocks, our souls
    were cased with steel,
And the hardships of that summer would nearly
    make us reel.
While skinning the damned old stinkers our lives
    they had no show,
For the Indians waited to pick us off on the hills of
    Mexico.

The season being near over, old Crego he did say
The crowd had been extravagant, was in debt to
    him that day, —
We coaxed him and we begged him and still it was
    no go,—
We left old Crego's bones to bleach on the range of
    the buffalo.

Oh, it's now we've crossed Pease River and homeward we are bound,

No more in that hell-fired country shall ever we be found.

Go home to our wives and sweethearts, tell others not to go,

For God's forsaken the buffalo range and the damned old buffalo.

Range of the Buffalo

'Twas in the town of Jacksbo - ro, In eigh-teen eigh - ty-three, When a man by the name of Cre - go... Came step-ping up to me; Say- ing, "How do you do, young

fel - low, And how would you like to go.. And

spend one summer sea-son On the range of the Buf - fa - lo?"

MACAFFIE'S CONFESSION

NOW come young men and list to me,
   A sad and mournful history;
And may you ne'er forgetful be
Of what I tell this day to thee.

Oh, I was thoughtless, young, and gay
And often broke the Sabbath day,
In wickedness I took delight
And sometimes done what wasn't right.

I'd scarcely passed my fifteenth year,
My mother and my father dear
Were silent in their deep, dark grave,
Their spirits gone to Him who gave.

'Twas on a pleasant summer day
When from my home I ran away
And took unto myself a wife,
Which step was fatal to my life.

Oh, she was kind and good to me
As ever woman ought to be,
And might this day have been alive no doubt,
Had I not met Miss Hatty Stout.

Ah, well I mind the fatal day
When Hatty stole my heart away;

'Twas love for her controlled my will
And did cause me my wife to kill.

'Twas on a brilliant summer's night
When all was still; the stars shone bright.
My wife lay still upon the bed
And I approached to her and said:

" Dear wife, here's medicine I've brought,
For you this day, my love, I've bought.
I know it will be good for you
For those vile fits,— pray take it, do."

She cast on me a loving look
And in her mouth the poison took;
Down by her infant on the bed
In her last, long sleep she laid her head.

Oh, who could tell a mother's thought
When first to her the news was brought;
The sheriff said her son was sought
And into prison must be brought.

Only a mother standing by
To hear them tell the reason why
Her son in prison, he must lie
Till on the scaffold he must die.

My father, sixty years of age,
The best of counsel did engage,

To see if something could be done
To save his disobedient son.

So, farewell, mother, do not weep,
Though soon with demons I will sleep,
My soul now feels its mental hell
And soon with demons I will dwell.

. . . .

The sheriff cut the slender cord,
His soul went up to meet its Lord;
The doctor said, " The wretch is dead,
His spirit from his body's fled."

His weeping mother cried aloud,
" O God, do save this gazing crowd,
That none may ever have to pay
For gambling on the Sabbath day."

LITTLE JOE, THE WRANGLER

IT'S little Joe, the wrangler, he'll wrangle never
    more,
His days with the *remuda* they are o'er;
'Twas a year ago last April when he rode into our
    camp,—
Just a little Texas stray and all alone,—
On a little Texas pony he called " Chaw."
With his brogan shoes and overalls, a tougher kid
You never in your life before had saw.

His saddle was a Texas " kak," built many years
    ago,
With an O. K. spur on one foot lightly swung;
His " hot roll " in a cotton sack so loosely tied be-
    hind,
And his canteen from his saddle-horn was swung.
He said that he had to leave his home, his pa had
    married twice;
And his new ma whipped him every day or two;
So he saddled up old Chaw one night and lit a shuck
    this way,
And he's now trying to paddle his own canoe.

He said if we would give him work, he'd do the best
    he could,
Though he didn't know straight up about a cow;

So the boss he cut him out a mount and kindly put
     him on,
For he sorta liked this little kid somehow.
Learned him to wrangle horses and to try to know
     them all,
And get them in at daylight if he could;
To follow the chuck-wagon and always hitch the
     team,
And to help the *cocinero* rustle wood.

We had driven to the Pecos, the weather being fine;
We had camped on the south side in a bend;
When a norther commenced blowin', we had doubled
     up our guard,
For it taken all of us to hold them in.
Little Joe, the wrangler, was called out with the rest;
Though the kid had scarcely reached the herd,
When the cattle they stampeded, like a hailstorm
     long they fled,
Then we were all a-ridin' for the lead.

'Midst the streaks of lightin' a horse we could see in
     the lead,
'Twas Little Joe, the wrangler, in the lead;
He was riding Old Blue Rocket with a slicker o'er
     his head,
A tryin' to check the cattle in their speed.
At last we got them milling and kinda quieted down,
And the extra guard back to the wagon went;

But there was one a-missin' and we knew it at a
glance,
'Twas our little Texas stray, poor Wrangling Joe.

The next morning just at day break, we found where
Rocket fell,
Down in a washout twenty feet below;
And beneath the horse, mashed to a pulp,— his spur
had rung the knell,—
Was our little Texas stray, poor Wrangling Joe.

Little Joe, The Wrangler

Lit - tle Joe, the wran-gler, He'll wran - gle nev - er-more,
rode up to our herd

His days with the re - mu - da they are o'er;
On a lit - tle Tex - as Po - ny he call'd Chaw;

'Twas a year a - go last A - pril he rode in - to our herd;
With his bro - gan shoes and o - veralls, a tough-er look-in' kid

Little Joe, The Wrangler—*Concluded*

Just a lit-tle Tex-as stray, and all a-lone.

You.. nev-er in your life be-fore had saw.

It was late in the eve-ning he

HARRY BALE

COME all kind friends and kindred dear and
      Christians young and old,
A story I'll relate to you, 'twill make your blood run
    cold;
'Tis all about an unfortunate boy who lived not far
    from here,
In the township of Arcade in the County of Lapeer.
It seems his occupation was a sawyer in a mill,
He followed it successfully two years, one month,
    until,
Until this fatal accident that caused many to weep
    and wail;
'Twas where this young man lost his life,— his name
    was Harry Bale.

On the 29th of April in the year of seventy-nine,
He went to work as usual, no fear did he design;
In lowering of the feed bar throwing the carriage
    into gear
It brought him down upon the saw and cut him quite
    severe;
It cut him through the collar-bone and half way
    down the back,
It threw him down upon the saw, the carriage com-
    ing back.

He started for the shanty, his strength was failing
    fast;
He said, " Oh, boys, I'm wounded: I fear it is my
    last."

His brothers they were sent for, likewise his sisters
    too,
The doctors came and dressed his wound, but kind
    words proved untrue.
Poor Harry had no father to weep beside his bed,
No kind and loving mother to sooth his aching head.
He was just as gallant a young man as ever you
    wished to know,
But he withered like a flower, it was his time to go.

They placed him in his coffin and laid him in his
    grave;
His brothers and sisters mourned the loss of a
    brother so true and brave.
They took him to the graveyard and laid him away
    to rest,
His body lies mouldering, his soul is among the blest.

FOREMAN MONROE

COME all you brave young shanty boys, and list
      while I relate
Concerning a young shanty boy and his untimely
      fate;
Concerning a young river man, so manly, true and
      brave;
'Twas on a jam at Gerry's Rock he met his watery
      grave;

'Twas on a Sunday morning as you will quickly hear,
Our logs were piled up mountain high, we could not
      keep them clear.
Our foreman said, " Come on, brave boys, with
      hearts devoid of fear,
We'll break the jam on Gerry's Rock and for Agons-
      town we'll steer."

Now, some of them were willing, while others they
      were not,
All for to work on Sunday they did not think they
      ought;
But six of our brave shanty boys had volunteered
      to go
And break the jam on Gerry's Rock with their fore-
      man, young Monroe.

They had not rolled off many logs 'till they heard
     his clear voice say,
" I'd have you boys be on your guard, for the jam
     will soon give way."
These words he'd scarcely spoken when the jam did
     break and go,
Taking with it six of those brave boys and their
     foreman, young Monroe.

Now when those other shanty boys this sad news
     came to hear,
In search of their dead comrades to the river they
     did steer;
Six of their mangled bodies a-floating down did go,
While crushed and bleeding near the banks lay the
     foreman, young Monroe.

They took him from his watery grave, brushed back
     his raven hair;
There was a fair form among them whose cries did
     rend the air;
There was a fair form among them, a girl from Sag-
     inaw town,
Whose cries rose to the skies for her lover who'd
     gone down.

Fair Clara was a noble girl, the river-man's true
     friend;
She and her widowed mother lived at the river's
     bend;

And the wages of her own true love the boss to her
    did pay,
But the shanty boys for her made up a generous sum
    next day.

They buried him quite decently; 'twas on the first
    of May;
Come all you brave young shanty boys and for your
    comrade pray.
Engraved upon the hemlock tree that by the grave
    does grow
Is the aged date and the sad fate of the foreman,
    young Monroe.

Fair Clara did not long survive, her heart broke
    with her grief;
And less than three months afterwards Death came
    to her relief;
And when the time had come and she was called
    to go,
Her last request was granted, to be laid by young
    Monroe.

Come all you brave young shanty boys, I'd have you
    call and see
Two green graves by the river side where grows a
    hemlock tree;
The shanty boys cut off the wood where lay those
    lovers low,—
'Tis the handsome Clara Vernon and her true love,
    Jack Monroe.

THE DREARY BLACK HILLS

KIND friends, you must pity my horrible tale,
 I am an object of pity, I am looking quite stale,
I gave up my trade selling Right's Patent Pills
To go hunting gold in the dreary Black Hills.

> Don't go away, stay at home if you can,
> Stay away from that city, they call it Cheyenne,
> For big Walipe or Comanche Bills
> They will lift up your hair on the dreary Black
>   Hills.

The round-house in Cheyenne is filled every night
With loafers and bummers of most every plight;
On their backs is no clothes, in their pockets no bills,
Each day they keep starting for the dreary Black
    Hills.

I got to Cheyenne, no gold could I find,
I thought of the lunch route I'd left far behind;
Through rain, hail, and snow, frozen plumb to the
    gills,—
They call me the orphan of the dreary Black Hills.

Kind friend, to conclude, my advice I'll unfold,
Don't go to the Black Hills a-hunting for gold;
Railroad speculators their pockets you'll fill
By taking a trip to those dreary Black Hills.

The Dreary Black Hills

Don't go away, stay at home if you can,
Stay away from that city, they call it Cheyenne,
For old Sitting Bull or Comanche Bills
They will take off your scalp on the dreary Black
  Hills.

The Dreary Black Hills

Kind friends, you must pit - y my hor - ri - ble tale,

I'm an ob - ject of pit - y, I'm look- ing quite stale;

I gave up my trade, Selling Right's Pat - ent Pills,

To go hunt-ing gold in the drear-y Black Hills.

REFRAIN

Don't go a - way, stay at home if you can;

Stay a-way from that cit - y they call it Chey-enne;

The Dreary Black Hills—*Concluded*

For big Wal - i - pee or Co - man - che Bills,

They will lift up your hair On the drear - y Black Hills.

A MORMON SONG

I USED to live on Cottonwood and owned a little
farm,
I was called upon a mission that gave me much alarm;
The reason that they called me, I'm sure I do not
know.
But to hoe the cane and cotton, straightway I must
go.

I yoked up Jim and Baldy, all ready for the start;
To leave my farm and garden, it almost broke my
heart;
But at last we got started, I cast a look behind,
For the sand and rocks of Dixie were running
through my mind.

Now, when we got to Black Ridge, my wagon it
broke down,
And I, being no carpenter and forty miles from
town,—
I cut a clumsy cedar and rigged an awkward slide,
But the wagon ran so heavy poor Betsy couldn't ride.

While Betsy was out walking I told her to take care,
When all of a sudden she struck a prickly pear,
Then she began to hollow as loud as she could
bawl,—
If I were back in Cottonwood, I wouldn't go at all.

Now, when we got to Sand Ridge, we couldn't go at
    all,
Old Jim and old Baldy began to puff and loll,
I cussed and swore a little, for I couldn't make the
    route,
For the team and I and Betsy were all of us played
    out.

At length we got to Washington; I thought we'd
    stay a while
To see if the flowers would make their virgin smile,
But I was much mistaken, for when we went away
The red hills of September were just the same in
    May.

It is so very dreary, there's nothing here to cheer,
But old pathetic sermons we very often hear;
They preach them by the dozens and prove them by
    the book,
But I'd sooner have a roasting-ear and stay at home
    and cook.

I am so awful weary I'm sure I'm almost dead;
'Tis six long weeks last Sunday since I have tasted
    bread;
Of turnip-tops and lucerne greens I've had enough
    to eat,
But I'd like to change my diet to buckwheat cakes
    and meat.

A Mormon Song

I had to sell my wagon for sorghum seed and bread;
Old Jim and old Baldy have long since been dead.
There 's no one left but me and Bet to hoe the cotton
    tree,—
God pity any Mormon that attempts to follow me!

THE BUFFALO HUNTERS

COME all you pretty girls, to you these lines I'll
write,
We are going to the range in which we take delight;
We are going on the range as we poor hunters do,
And the tender-footed fellows can stay at home with
you.

It's all of the day long as we go tramping round
In search of the buffalo that we may shoot him
down;
Our guns upon our shoulders, our belts of forty
rounds,
We send them up Salt River to some happy hunting
grounds.

Our game, it is the antelope, the buffalo, wolf, and
deer,
Who roam the wide prairies without a single fear;
We rob him of his robe and think it is no harm,
To buy us food and clothing to keep our bodies
warm.

The buffalo, he is the noblest of the band,
He sometimes rejects in throwing up his hand.
His shaggy main thrown forward, his head raised
to the sky,

He seems to say, " We're coming, boys; so hunter,
mind your eye."

Our fires are made of mesquite roots, our beds are
on the ground;
Our houses made of buffalo hides, we make them
tall and round;
Our furniture is the camp kettle, the coffee pot, and
pan,
Our chuck it is both bread and meat, mingled well
with sand.

Our neighbors are the Cheyennes, the 'Rapahoes, and
Sioux,
Their mode of navigation is a buffalo-hide canoe.
And when they come upon you they take you un-
aware,
And such a peculiar way they have of raising
hunter's hair.

THE LITTLE OLD SOD SHANTY

I AM looking rather seedy now, while holding
    down my claim,
And my victuals are not always served the best;
And the mice play shyly round me as I nestle down
    to rest
In my little old sod shanty on my claim.

    The hinges are of leather and the windows have
        no glass,
    While the board roof lets the howling blizzards in,
    And I hear the hungry cayote as he slinks up
        through the grass
    Round the little old sod shanty on my claim.

Yet, I rather like the novelty of living in this way,
Though my bill of fare is always rather tame,
But I'm happy as a clam on the land of Uncle Sam
In the little old sod shanty on my claim.

But when I left my Eastern home, a bachelor so
    gay,
To try and win my way to wealth and fame,
I little thought I'd come down to burning twisted
    hay
In the little old sod shanty on my claim.

The Little Old Sod Shanty

My clothes are plastered o'er with dough, I'm look-
    ing like a fright,
And everything is scattered round the room,
But I wouldn't give the freedom that I have out in
    the West
For the table of the Eastern man's old home.

Still, I wish that some kind-hearted girl would pity
    on me take
And relieve me from the mess that I am in;
The angel, how I'd bless her if this her home she'd
    make
In the little old sod shanty on my claim.

And we would make our fortunes on the prairies of
    the West,
Just as happy as two lovers we'd remain;
We'd forget the trials and troubles we endured at
    the first
In the little old sod shanty on my claim.

And if fate should bless us with now and then an
    heir
To cheer our hearts with honest pride of fame,
Oh, then we'd be contented for the toil that we had
    spent
In the little old sod shanty on our claim.

When time enough had lapsed and all those little
    brats

The Little Old Sod Shanty

To noble man and womanhood had grown,
It wouldn't seem half so lonely as round us we should
look
And we'd see the old sod shanty on our claim.

THE GOL-DARNED WHEEL

I CAN take the wildest bronco in the tough old
    woolly West.
I can ride him, I can break him, let him do his level
    best;
I can handle any cattle ever wore a coat of hair,
And I've had a lively tussle with a tarnel grizzly
    bear.
I can rope and throw the longhorn of the wildest
    Texas brand,
And in Indian disagreements I can play a leading
    hand,
But at last I got my master and he surely made me
    squeal
When the boys got me a-straddle of that gol-darned
    wheel.

It was at the Eagle Ranch, on the Brazos,
When I first found that darned contrivance that
    upset me in the dust.
A tenderfoot had brought it, he was wheeling all
    the way
From the sun-rise end of freedom out to San Fran-
    cisco Bay.
He tied up at the ranch for to get outside a meal,
Never thinking we would monkey with his gol-
    darned wheel.

The Gol-Darned Wheel

Arizona Jim begun it when he said to Jack McGill
There was fellows forced to limit bragging on their
    riding skill,
And he'd venture the admission the same fellow that
    he meant
Was a very handy cutter far as riding bronchos went;
But he would find that he was bucking 'gainst a dif-
    ferent kind of deal
If he threw his leather leggins 'gainst a gol-darned
    wheel.

Such a slam against my talent made me hotter than
    a mink,
And I swore that I would ride him for amusement
    or for chink.
And it was nothing but a plaything for the kids and
    such about,
And they'd have their ideas shattered if they'd lead
    the critter out.
They held it while I mounted and gave the word
    to go;
The shove they gave to start me warn't unreasonably
    slow.
But I never spilled a cuss word and I never spilled a
    squeal —
I was building reputation on that gol-darned wheel.

Holy Moses and the Prophets, how we split the
    Texas air,

And the wind it made whip-crackers of my same old
    canthy hair,
And I sorta comprehended as down the hill we went
There was bound to be a smash-up that I couldn't
    well prevent.
Oh, how them punchers bawled, " Stay with her,
    Uncle Bill!
Stick your spurs in her, you sucker! turn her muzzle
    up the hill! "
But I never made an answer, I just let the cusses
    squeal,
I was finding reputation on that gol-darned wheel.

The grade was mighty sloping from the ranch down
    to the creek
And I went a-galliflutin' like a crazy lightning
    streak,—
Went whizzing and a-darting first this way and then
    that,
The darned contrivance sort o' wobbling like the
    flying of a bat.
I pulled upon the handles, but I couldn't check it up,
And I yanked and sawed and hollowed but the
    darned thing wouldn't stop.
Then a sort of a meachin' in my brain began to
    steal,
That the devil held a mortgage on that gol-darned
    wheel.

I've a sort of dim and hazy remembrance of the
    stop,
With the world a-goin' round and the stars all tan-
    gled up;
Then there came an intermission that lasted till I
    found
I was lying at the ranch with the boys all gathered
    round,
And a doctor was a-sewing on the skin where it was
    ripped,
And old Arizona whispered, " Well, old boy, I guess
    you're whipped,"
And I told him I was busted from sombrero down to
    heel,
And he grinned and said, " You ought to see that
    gol-darned wheel."

BONNIE BLACK BESS

WHEN fortune's blind goddess
    Had fled my abode,
And friends proved unfaithful,
I took to the road;
To plunder the wealthy
And relieve my distress,
I bought you to aid me,
My Bonnie Black Bess.

No vile whip nor spur
Did your sides ever gall,
For none did you need,
You would bound at my call;
And for each act of kindness
You would me caress,
Thou art never unfaithful,
My Bonnie Black Bess.

When dark, sable midnight
Her mantle had thrown
O'er the bright face of nature,
How oft we have gone
To the famed Houndslow heath,
Though an unwelcome guest
To the minions of fortune,
My Bonnie Black Bess.

Bonnie Black Bess

How silent you stood
When the carriage I stopped,
The gold and the jewels
Its inmates would drop.
No poor man I plundered
Nor e'er did oppress
The widows or orphans,
My Bonnie Black Bess.

When Argus-eyed justice
Did me hot pursue,
From Yorktown to London
Like lightning we flew.
No toll bars could stop you,
The waters did breast,
And in twelve hours we made it,
My Bonnie Black Bess.

But hate darkens o'er me,
Despair is my lot,
And the law does pursue me
For the many I've shot;
To save me, poor brute,
Thou hast done thy best,
Thou art worn out and weary,
My Bonnie Black Bess.

Hark! they never shall have
A beast like thee;
So noble and gentle

And brave, thou must die,
My dumb friend,
Though it does me distress,—
There! There! I have shot thee,
My Bonnie Black Bess.

In after years
When I am dead and gone,
This story will be handed
From father to son;
My fate some will pity,
And some will confess
'Twas through kindness I killed thee,
My Bonnie Black Bess.

No one can e'er say
That ingratitude dwelt
In the bosom of Turpin,—
'Twas a vice never felt.
I will die like a man
And soon be at rest;
Now, farewell forever,
My Bonnie Black Bess.

THE LAST LONGHORN

AN ancient long-horned bovine
 Lay dying by the river;
There was lack of vegetation
And the cold winds made him shiver;
A cowboy sat beside him
With sadness in his face,
To see his final passing,—
This last of a noble race.

The ancient eunuch struggled
And raised his shaking head,
Saying, " I care not to linger
When all my friends are dead.
These Jerseys and these Holsteins,
They are no friends of mine;
They belong to the nobility
Who live across the brine.

" Tell the Durhams and the Herefords
When they come a-grazing round,
And see me lying stark and stiff
Upon the frozen ground,
I don't want them to bellow
When they see that I am dead,
For I was born in Texas
Near the river that is Red.

" Tell the cayotes, when they come at night
    A-hunting for their prey,
They might as well go further,
    For they'll find it will not pay.
If they attempt to eat me,
    They very soon will see
That my bones and hide are petrified,—
    They'll find no beef on me.

" I remember back in the seventies,
    Full many summers past,
There was grass and water plenty,
    But it was too good to last.
I little dreamed what would happen
    Some twenty summers hence,
When the nester came with his wife, his kids,
    His dogs, and his barbed-wire fence."

His voice sank to a murmur,
    His breath was short and quick;
The cowboy tried to skin him
    When he saw he couldn't kick;
He rubbed his knife upon his boot
    Until he made it shine,
But he never skinned old longhorn,
    Caze he couldn't cut his rine.

And the cowboy riz up sadly
    'And mounted his cayuse,

198

The Last Longhorn

Saying, " The time has come when longhorns
And their cowboys are no use!"
And while gazing sadly backward
Upon the dead bovine,
His bronc stepped in a dog-hole
And fell and broke his spine.

The cowboys and the longhorns
Who partnered in eighty-four
Have gone to their last round-up
Over on the other shore;
They answered well their purpose,
But their glory must fade and go,
Because men say there's better things
In the modern cattle show.

A PRISONER FOR LIFE

FARE you well, green fields,
   Soft meadows, adieu!
Rocks and mountains,
I depart from you;
Nevermore shall my eyes
By your beauties be blest,
Nevermore shall you soothe
My sad bosom to rest.

Farewell, little birdies,
That fly in the sky,
You fly all day long
And sing your troubles by;
I am doomed to this cell,
I heave a deep sigh;
My heart sinks within me,
In anguish I die.

Fare you well, little fishes,
That glides through the sea,
Your life's all sunshine,
All light, and all glee;
Nevermore shall I watch
Your skill in the wave,
I'll depart from all friends
This side of the grave.

A Prisoner for Life

What would I give
Such freedom to share,
To roam at my ease
And breathe the fresh air;
I would roam through the cities,
Through village and dell,
But I never would return
To my cold prison cell.

What's life without liberty?
I ofttimes have said,
Of a poor troubled mind
That's always in dread;
No sun, moon, and stars
Can on me now shine,
No change in my danger
From daylight till dawn.

Fare you well, kind friends,
I am willing to own,
Such a wild outcast
Never was known;
I'm the downfall of my family,
My children, my wife;
God pity and pardon
The poor prisoner for life.

A Prisoner For Life

Fare you well green fields,.. Soft mead-ows, a - dieu!

Rocks and moun-tains I de - part.... from you,

Nev - er- more shall my eyes by your beau-ties be fed,

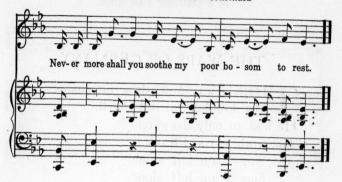

Nev-er more shall you soothe my poor bo-som to rest.

THE WARS OF GERMANY

THERE was a wealthy merchant,
   In London he did dwell,
He had an only daughter,
The truth to you I'll tell.
     Sing I am left alone,
     Sing I am left alone.

She was courted by a lord
Of very high degree,
She was courted by a sailor Jack
Just from the wars of Germany.
     Sing I am left alone,
     Sing I am left alone.

Her parents came to know this,
That such a thing could be,
A sailor Jack, a sailor lad,
Just from the wars of Germany.
     Sing I am left alone,
     Sing I am left alone.

So Polly she's at home
With money at command,
She taken a notion
To view some foreign land.
     Sing I am left alone,
     Sing I am left alone.

She went to the tailor's shop
And dressed herself in man's array,
And was off to an officer
To carry her straight away.
    Sing I am left alone,
    Sing I am left alone.

" Good morning," says the officer,
  And " Morning," says she,
" Here's fifty guineas if you'll carry me
  To the wars of Germany."
    Sing I am left alone,
    Sing I am left alone.

" Your waist is too slender,
  Your fingers are too small,
I am afraid from your countenance
  You can't face a cannon ball."
    Sing I am left alone,
    Sing I am left alone.

" My waist is not too slender,
  My fingers are not too small,
And never would I quiver
  To face a cannon ball."
    Sing I am left alone,
    Sing I am left alone.

" We don't often 'list an officer
  Unless the name we know; "

She answered him in a low, sweet voice,
" You may call me Jack Munro."
    Sing I am left alone,
    Sing I am left alone.

We gathered up our men
And quickly we did sail,
We landed in France
With a sweet and pleasant gale.
    Sing I am left alone,
    Sing I am left alone.

We were walking on the land,
Up and down the line,—
Among the dead and wounded
Her own true love she did find.
    Sing I am left alone,
    Sing I am left alone.

She picked him up all in her arms,
To Tousen town she went;
She soon found a doctor
To dress and heal his wounds,
    Sing I am left alone,
    Sing I am left alone.

So Jacky, he is married,
And his bride by his side,
In spite of her old parents
And all the world beside.
    Sing no longer left alone,
    Sing no longer left alone.

FREIGHTING FROM WILCOX TO GLOBE

COME all you jolly freighters
    That has freighted on the road,
That has hauled a load of freight
From Wilcox to Globe;
We freighted on this road
For sixteen years or more
A-hauling freight for Livermore,—
No wonder that I'm poor.

    And it's home, dearest home;
    And it's home you ought to be,
    Over on the Gila
    In the white man's country,
    Where the poplar and the ash
    And mesquite will ever be
    Growing green down on the Gila;
    There's a home for you and me.

'Twas in the spring of seventy-three
I started with my team,
Led by false illusion
And those foolish, golden dreams;
The first night out from Wilcox
My best wheel horse was stole,
And it makes me curse a little
To come out in the hole.

207

This then only left me three,—
Kit, Mollie and old Mike;
Mike being the best one of the three
I put him out on spike;
I then took the mountain road
So the people would not smile,
And it took fourteen days
To travel thirteen mile.

But I got there all the same
With my little three-up spike;
It taken all my money, then,
To buy a mate for Mike.
You all know how it is
When once you get behind,
You never get even again
Till you damn steal them blind.

I was an honest man
When I first took to the road,
I would not swear an oath,
Nor would I tap a load;
But now you ought to see my mules
When I begin to cuss,
They flop their ears and wiggle their tails
And pull the load or bust.

Now I can tap a whiskey barrel
With nothing but a stick,
No one can detect me
I've got it down so slick;

Just fill it up with water,—
Sure, there's no harm in that.

Now my clothes are not the finest,
Nor are they genteel;
But they will have to do me
Till I can make another steal.
My boots are number elevens,
For I swiped them from a chow,
And my coat cost dos reals
From a little Apache squaw.

Now I have freighted in the sand,
I have freighted in the rain,
I have bogged my wagons down
And dug them out again;
I have worked both late and early
Till I was almost dead,
And I have spent some nights sleeping
In an Arizona bed.

Now barbed wire and bacon
Is all that they will pay,
But you have to show your copper checks
To get your grain and hay;
If you ask them for five dollars,
Old Meyers will scratch his pate,
And the clerks in their white, stiff collars
Say, " Get down and pull your freight."

But I want to die and go to hell,
Get there before Livermore and Meyers
And get a job of hauling coke
To keep up the devil's fires;
If I get the job of singeing them,
I'll see they don't get free;
I'll treat them like a yaller dog,
As they have treated me.

And it's home, dearest home;
And it's home you ought to be,
Over on the Gila,
In the white man's country,
Where the poplar and the ash
And mesquite will ever be
Growing green down on the Gila;
There's a home for you and me.

THE ARIZONA BOYS AND GIRLS

COME all of you people, I pray you draw near,
   A comical ditty you all shall hear.
The boys in this country they try to advance
By courting the ladies and learning to dance,—
And they're down, down, and they're down.

The boys in this country they try to be plain,
Those words that you hear you may hear them again,
With twice as much added on if you can.
There's many a boy stuck up for a man,—
And they're down, down, and they're down.

They will go to their parties, their whiskey they'll
      take,
And out in the dark their bottles they'll break;
You'll hear one say, " There's a bottle around here;
So come around, boys, and we'll all take a share,"—
And they're down, down, and they're down.

There is some wears shoes and some wears boots,
But there are very few that rides who don't shoot;
More than this, I'll tell you what they'll do,
They'll get them a watch and a ranger hat, too,—
And they're down, down, and they're down.

They'll go in the hall with spurs on their heel,
They'll get them a partner to dance the next reel,

Saying, " How do I look in my new brown suit,
With my pants stuffed down in the top of my
    boot? "—
And they're down, down, and they're down.

Now I think it's quite time to leave off these lads
For here are some girls that's fully as bad;
They'll trim up their dresses and curl up their hair,
And like an old owl before the glass they'll stare,—
And they're down, down, and they're down.

The girls in the country they grin like a cat,
And with giggling and laughing they don't know
    what they're at,
They think they're pretty and I tell you they're wise,
But they couldn't get married to save their two
    eyes,—
And they're down, down, and they're down.

You can tell a good girl wherever she's found;
No trimming, no lace, no nonsense around;
With a long-eared bonnet tied under her chin,—
.   .   .   .
And they're down, down, and they're down.

They'll go to church with their snuff-box in hand,
They'll give it a tap to make it look grand;
Perhaps there is another one or two
And they'll pass it around and it's " Madam, won't
    you,"—
And they're down, down, and they're down.

Now, I think it's quite time for this ditty to end;
If there's anyone here that it will offend,
If there's anyone here that thinks it amiss
Just come around now and give the singer a kiss,—
And they're down, down, and they're down.

THE DYING RANGER

THE sun was sinking in the west
  And fell with lingering ray
Through the branches of a forest
Where a wounded ranger lay;
Beneath the shade of a palmetto
And the sunset silvery sky,
Far away from his home in Texas
They laid him down to die.

A group had gathered round him,
His comrades in the fight,
A tear rolled down each manly cheek
As he bid a last good-night.
One tried and true companion
Was kneeling by his side,
To stop his life-blood flowing,
But alas, in vain he tried.

When to stop the life-blood flowing
He found 'twas all in vain,
The tears rolled down each man's cheek
Like light showers of rain.
Up spoke the noble ranger,
" Boys, weep no more for me,
I am crossing the deep waters
To a country that is free.

The Dying Ranger

"Draw closer to me, comrades,
  And listen to what I say,
I am going to tell a story
  While my spirit hastens away.
Way back in Northwest Texas,
  That good old Lone Star state,
There is one that for my coming
  With a weary heart will wait.

"A fair young girl, my sister,
  My only joy, my pride,
She was my friend from boyhood,
  I had no one left beside.
I have loved her as a brother,
  And with a father's care
I have strove from grief and sorrow
  Her gentle heart to spare.

"My mother, she lies sleeping
  Beneath the church-yard sod,
And many a day has passed away
  Since her spirit fled to God.
My father, he lies sleeping
  Beneath the deep blue sea,
I have no other kindred,
  There are none but Nell and me.

"But our country was invaded
  And they called for volunteers;
She threw her arms around me,
  Then burst into tears,

215

Saying, ' Go, my darling brother,
Drive those traitors from our shore,
My heart may need your presence,
But our country needs you more.'

" It is true I love my country,
For her I gave my all.
If it hadn't been for my sister,
I would be content to fall.
I am dying, comrades, dying,
She will never see me more,
But in vain she'll wait my coming
By our little cabin door.

" Comrades, gather closer
And listen to my dying prayer.
Who will be to her as a brother,
And shield her with a brother's care?"
Up spake the noble rangers,
They answered one and all,
" We will be to her as brothers
Till the last one does fall."

One glad smile of pleasure
O'er the ranger's face was spread:
One dark, convulsive shadow,
And the ranger boy was dead.
Far from his darling sister
We laid him down to rest
With his saddle for a pillow
And his gun across his breast.

The Dying Ranger

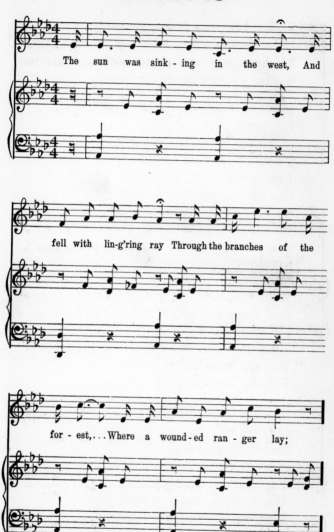

The sun was sink - ing in the west, And fell with lin-g'ring ray Through the branches of the for - est,... Where a wound-ed ran - ger lay;

The Dying Ranger—*Concluded*

'Neath the shade of a pal - met - to... And the sun - set sil - v'ry sky, Far a - way from his home in Tex - as,.... They laid him down to die.

THE FAIR FANNIE MOORE

YONDER stands a cottage,
  All deserted and alone,
Its paths are neglected,
With grass overgrown;
Go in and you will see
Some dark stains on the floor,—
Alas! it is the blood
Of fair Fannie Moore.

To Fannie, so blooming,
Two lovers they came;
One offered young Fannie
His wealth and his name;
But neither his money
Nor pride could secure
A place in the heart
Of fair Fannie Moore.

The first was young Randell,
So bold and so proud,
Who to the fair Fannie
His haughty head bowed;
But his wealth and his house
Both failed to allure
The heart from the bosom
Of fair Fannie Moore.

219

The next was young Henry,
Of lowest degree.
He won her fond love
And enraptured was he;
And then at the altar
He quick did secure
The hand with the heart
Of the fair Fannie Moore.

As she was alone
In her cottage one day,
When business had called
Her fond husband away,
Young Randell, the haughty,
Came in at the door
And clasped in his arms
The fair Fannie Moore.

" O Fannie, O Fannie,
Reflect on your fate
And accept of my offer
Before it's too late;
For one thing to-night
I am bound to secure,—
'Tis the love or the life
Of the fair Fannie Moore."

" Spare me, Oh, spare me! "
The young Fannie cries,
While the tears swiftly flow

From her beautiful eyes;
" Oh, no ! " cries young Randell,
" Go home to your rest,"
And he buried his knife
In her snowy white breast.

So Fannie, so blooming,
In her bright beauty died;
Young Randell, the haughty,
Was taken and tried;
At length he was hung
On a tree at the door,
For shedding the blood
Of the fair Fannie Moore.

Young Henry, the shepherd,
Distracted and wild,
Did wander away
From his own native isle.
Till at length, claimed by death,
He was brought to this shore
And laid by the side
Of the fair Fannie Moore.

HELL IN TEXAS

THE devil, we're told, in hell was chained,
 And a thousand years he there remained;
He never complained nor did he groan,
But determined to start a hell of his own,
Where he could torment the souls of men
Without being chained in a prison pen.
So he asked the Lord if he had on hand
Anything left when he made the land.

The Lord said, " Yes, I had plenty on hand,
But I left it down on the Rio Grande;
The fact is, old boy, the stuff is so poor
I don't think you could use it in hell anymore."
But the devil went down to look at the truck,
And said if it came as a gift he was stuck;
For after examining it carefully and well
He concluded the place was too dry for hell.

So, in order to get it off his hands,
The Lord promised the devil to water the lands;
For he had some water, or rather some dregs,
A regular cathartic that smelled like bad eggs.
Hence the deal was closed and the deed was given
And the Lord went back to his home in heaven.
And the devil then said, " I have all that is needed
To make a good hell," and hence he succeeded.

Hell in Texas

He began to put thorns in all of the trees,
And mixed up the sand with millions of fleas;
And scattered tarantulas along all the roads;
Put thorns on the cactus and horns on the toads.
He lengthened the horns of the Texas steers,
And put an addition on the rabbit's ears;
He put a little devil in the broncho steed,
And poisoned the feet of the centipede.

The rattlesnake bites you, the scorpion stings,
The mosquito delights you with buzzing wings;
The sand-burrs prevail and so do the ants,
And those who sit down need half-soles on their
    pants.
The devil then said that throughout the land
He'd managed to keep up the devil's own brand,
And all would be mavericks unless they bore
The marks of scratches and bites and thorns by the
    score.

The heat in the summer is a hundred and ten,
Too hot for the devil and too hot for men.
The wild boar roams through the black chaparral,—
It's a hell of a place he has for a hell.
The red pepper grows on the banks of the brook;
The Mexicans use it in all that they cook.
Just dine with a Greaser and then you will shout,
" I've hell on the inside as well as the out! "

BY MARKENTURA'S FLOWERY MARGE

BY Markentura's flowery marge the Red Chief's
     wigwam stood,
Before the white man's rifle rang, loud echoing
     through the wood;
The tommy-hawk and scalping knife together lay at
     rest,
And peace was in the forest shade and in the red
     man's breast.

Oh, the Spotted Fawn, oh, the Spotted Fawn,
The life and light of the forest shade,—
The Red Chief's child is gone!

By Markentura's flowery marge the Spotted Fawn
     had birth
And grew as fair an Indian maid as ever graced the
     earth.
She was the Red Chief's only child and sought by
     many a brave,
But to the gallant young White Cloud her plighted
     troth she gave.

By Markentura's flowery marge the bridal song
     arose,
Nor dreamed they in that festive night of near ap-
     proaching woes;

But through the forest stealthily the white man came
    in wrath,
And fiery darts before them spread, and death was
    in their path.

By Markentura's flowery marge next morn no strife
    was seen,
But a wail went up, for the young Fawn's blood and
    White Cloud's dyed the green.
A burial in their own rude way the Indians gave them
    there,
And a low sweet requiem the brook sang and the air.

    Oh, the Spotted Fawn, oh, the Spotted Fawn,
    The life and light of the forest shade,—
    The Red Chief's child is gone!

THE STATE OF ARKANSAW

MY name is Stamford Barnes, I come from
    Nobleville town;
I've traveled this wide world over, I've traveled this
    wide world round.
I've met with ups and downs in life but better days
    I've saw,
But I've never knew what misery were till I came to
    Arkansaw.

I landed in St. Louis with ten dollars and no more;
I read the daily papers till both my eyes were sore;
I read them evening papers until at last I saw
Ten thousand men were wanted in the state of Arkan-
    saw.

I wiped my eyes with great surprise when I read this
    grateful news,
And straightway off I started to see the agent, Billy
    Hughes.
He says, " Pay me five dollars and a ticket to you
    I'll draw,
It'll land you safe upon the railroad in the State of
    Arkansaw."

I started off one morning a quarter after five;
I started from St. Louis, half dead and half alive;

I bought me a quart of whiskey my misery to thaw,
I got as drunk as a biled owl when I left for old
    Arkansaw.

I landed in Ft. Smith one sultry Sunday afternoon,
It was in the month of May, the early month of June,
Up stepped a walking skeleton with a long and lan-
    tern jaw,
Invited me to his hotel, " The best in Arkansaw."

I followed my conductor into his dwelling place;
Poverty were depictured in his melancholy face.
His bread it was corn dodger, his beef I could not
    chaw;
This was the kind of hash they fed me in the State
    of Arkansaw.

I started off next morning to catch the morning train,
He says to me, " You'd better work, for I have some
    land to drain.
I'll pay you fifty cents a day, your board, washing,
    and all,—
You'll find yourself a different man when you leave
    old Arkansaw."

I worked six weeks for the son of a gun, Jesse Her-
    ring was his name,
He was six foot seven in his stocking feet and taller
    than any crane;

His hair hung down in strings over his long and lan-
 tern jaw,—
He was a photograph of all the gents who lived in
 Arkansaw.

He fed me on corn dodgers as hard as any rock,
Until my teeth began to loosen and my knees began
 to knock;
I got so thin on sassafras tea I could hide behind a
 straw,
And indeed I was a different man when I left old
 Arkansaw.

Farewell to swamp angels, cane brakes, and chills;
Farewell to sage and sassafras and corn dodger pills.
If ever I see this land again, I'll give to you my paw;
It will be through a telescope from here to Arkansaw.

THE TEXAS COWBOY

OH, I am a Texas cowboy,
  Far away from home,
If ever I get back to Texas
I never more will roam.

Montana is too cold for me
And the winters are too long;
Before the round-ups do begin
Our money is all gone.

Take this old hen-skin bedding,
Too thin to keep me warm,—
I nearly freeze to death, my boys,
Whenever there's a storm.

And take this old " tarpoleon,"
Too thin to shield my frame,—
I got it down in Nebraska
A-dealin' a Monte game.

Now to win these fancy leggins
I'll have enough to do;
They cost me twenty dollars
The day that they were new.

I have an outfit on the Mussel Shell,
But that I'll never see,

Unless I get sent to represent
The Circle or D. T.

I've worked down in Nebraska
Where the grass grows ten feet high,
And the cattle are such rustlers
That they seldom ever die;

I've worked up in the sand hills
And down upon the Platte,
Where the cowboys are good fellows
And the cattle always fat;

I've traveled lots of country,—
Nebraska's hills of sand,
Down through the Indian Nation,
And up the Rio Grande;—

But the Bad Lands of Montana
Are the worst I ever seen,
The cowboys are all tenderfeet
And the dogies are too lean.

If you want to see some bad lands,
Go over on the Dry;
You will bog down in the coulees
Where the mountains reach the sky.

A tenderfoot to lead you
Who never knows the way,

The Texas Cowboy

You are playing in the best of luck
If you eat more than once a day.

Your grub is bread and bacon
And coffee black as ink;
The water is so full of alkali
It is hardly fit to drink.

They will wake you in the morning
Before the break of day,
And send you on a circle
A hundred miles away.

All along the Yellowstone
'Tis cold the year around;
You will surely get consumption
By sleeping on the ground.

Work in Montana
Is six months in the year;
When all your bills are settled
There is nothing left for beer.

Work down in Texas
Is all the year around;
You will never get consumption
By sleeping on the ground.

Come all you Texas cowboys
And warning take from me,

The Texas Cowboy

And do not go to Montana
To spend your money free.

But stay at home in Texas
Where work lasts the year around,
And you will never catch consumption
By sleeping on the ground.

THE DREARY, DREARY LIFE

A COWBOY'S life is a dreary, dreary life,
   Some say it's free from care;
Rounding up the cattle from morning till night
In the middle of the prairie so bare.

   Half-past four, the noisy cook will roar,
"Whoop-a-whoop-a-hey!"
   Slowly you will rise with sleepy-feeling eyes,
   The sweet, dreamy night passed away.

The greener lad he thinks it's play,
He'll soon peter out on a cold rainy day,
With his big bell spurs and his Spanish hoss,
He'll swear to you he was once a boss.

The cowboy's life is a dreary, dreary life,
He's driven through the heat and cold;
While the rich man's a-sleeping on his velvet couch,
Dreaming of his silver and gold.

Spring-time sets in, double trouble will begin,
The weather is so fierce and cold;
Clothes are wet and frozen to our necks,
The cattle we can scarcely hold.

The cowboy's life is a dreary one,
He works all day to the setting of the sun;

The Dreary, Dreary Life

And then his day's work is not done,
For there's his night herd to go on.

The wolves and owls with their terrifying howls
Will disturb us in our midnight dream,
As we lie on our slickers on a cold, rainy night
Way over on the Pecos stream.

You are speaking of your farms, you are speaking of
your charms,
You are speaking of your silver and gold;
But a cowboy's life is a dreary, dreary life,
He's driven through the heat and cold.

Some folks say that we are free from care,
Free from all other harm;
But we round up the cattle from morning till night
Way over on the prairie so dry.

I used to run about, now I stay at home,
Take care of my wife and child;
Nevermore to roam, always stay at home,
Take care of my wife and child.

Half-past four the noisy cook will roar,
"Hurrah, boys! she's breaking day!"
Slowly we will rise and wipe our sleepy eyes,
The sweet, dreamy night passed away.

The Dreary, Dreary Life

A cow-boy's life is a drear-y, drear-y life, Some
REFRAIN.—Half-past four the.. noi-sy cook will roar,

say it's free from care;
"Whoop-a-whoop-a-hey!"
Rounding up the
Slow-ly you will

cat-tle from morn-ing till night In the
rise.... with sleep-y feel-ing eyes, The....

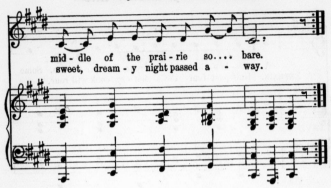

mid - dle   of   the   prai - rie   so.... bare.
sweet,   dream - y   night passed a - way.

JIM FARROW

IT'S Jim Farrow and John Farrow and little
    Simon, too,
Have plenty of cattle where I have but few.
Marking and branding both night and day,—
It's " Keep still, boys, my boys, and you'll all get your
    pay."
It's up to the courthouse, the first thing they know,
Before the Grand Jury they'll have to go.
They'll ask you about ear-marks, they'll ask you
    about brand,
But tell them you were absent when the work was
    on hand.
Jim Farrow brands J. F. on the side;
The next comes Johnnie who takes the whole hide;
Little Simon, too has H. on the loin; —
All stand for Farrow but it's not good for Sime.
You ask for the mark, I don't think it's fair,
You'll find the cow's head but the ear isn't there
It's a crop and a split and a sort of a twine,—
All stand for F. but it's not good for Sime.

" Get up, my boys," Jim Farrow will say,
" And out to horse hunting before it is day."
So we get up and are out on the way
But it's damn few horses we find before day.
" Now saddle your horses and out on the peaks

237

To see if the heifers are out on the creeks."
We'll round 'em to-day and we'll round 'em to-
    morrow,
And this ends my song concerning the Farrows.

YOUNG CHARLOTTIE

YOUNG Charlottie lived by a mountain side in
    a wild and lonely spot,
There was no village for miles around except her
    father's cot;
And yet on many a wintry night young boys would
    gather there,—
Her father kept a social board, and she was very
    fair.

One New Year's Eve as the sun went down, she cast
    a wistful eye
Out from the window pane as a merry sleigh went by.
At a village fifteen miles away was to be a ball that
    night;
Although the air was piercing cold, her heart was
    merry and light.

At last her laughing eye lit up as a well-known voice
    she heard,
And dashing in front of the door her lover's sleigh
    appeared.
" O daughter, dear," her mother said, " this blanket
    round you fold,
'Tis such a dreadful night abroad and you will catch
    your death of cold."

"Oh no, oh no!" young Charlottie cried, as she
laughed like a gipsy queen,
"To ride in blankets muffled up, I never would be
seen.
My silken coat is quite enough, you know it is lined
throughout,
And there is my silken scarf to wrap my head and
neck about."

Her bonnet and her gloves were on, she jumped into
the sleigh,
And swiftly slid down the mountain side and over
the hills away.
All muffled up so silent, five miles at last were past
When Charlie with few but shivering words, the
silence broke at last.

"Such a dreadful night I never saw, my reins I can
scarcely hold."
Young Charlottie then feebly said, "I am exceedingly
cold."
He cracked his whip and urged his speed much
faster than before,
While at least five other miles in silence had passed
o'er.

Spoke Charles, "How fast the freezing ice is gathering on my brow!"
Young Charlottie then feebly said, "I'm growing
warmer now."

So on they sped through the frosty air and the glittering cold starlight
Until at last the village lights and the ball-room came
in sight.

They reached the door and Charles sprang out and
reached his hands to her.
"Why sit you there like a monument that has no
power to stir?"
He called her once, he called her twice, she answered
not a word,
And then he called her once again but still she never
stirred.

He took her hand in his; 'twas cold and hard as any
stone.
He tore the mantle from her face while cold stars on
it shone.
Then quickly to the lighted hall her lifeless form
he bore; —
Young Charlottie's eyes were closed forever, her
voice was heard no more.

And there he sat down by her side while bitter tears
did flow,
And cried, " My own, my charming bride, you nevermore shall know."
He twined his arms around her neck and kissed her
marble brow,
And his thoughts flew back to where she said, " I'm
growing warmer now."

Young Charlottie

He took her back into the sleigh and quickly hurried
    home;
When he arrived at her father's door, oh, how her
    friends did mourn;
They mourned the loss of a daughter dear, while
    Charles wept over the gloom,
Till at last he died with the bitter grief,— now they
    both lie in one tomb.

THE SKEW-BALL BLACK

IT was down to Red River I came,
  Prepared to play a damned tough game,—
Whoa! skew, till I saddle you, whoa!

I crossed the river to the ranch where I intended to
    work,
With a big six-shooter and a derned good dirk,—
Whoa! skew, till I saddle you, whoa!

They roped me out a skew-ball black
With a double set-fast on his back,—
Whoa! skew, till I saddle you, whoa!

And when I was mounted on his back,
The boys all yelled, " Just give him slack,"—
Whoa! skew, till I saddle you, whoa!

They rolled and tumbled and yelled, by God,
For he threw me a-whirling all over the sod,—
Whoa! skew, till I saddle you, whoa!

I went to the boss and I told him I'd resign,
The fool tumbled over, and I thought he was dyin',—
Whoa! skew, till I saddle you, whoa!

And it's to Arkansaw I'll go back,
To hell with Texas and the skew-ball black,—
Whoa! skew, till I saddle you, whoa!

THE RAMBLING COWBOY

THERE was a rich old rancher who lived in the country by,
He had a lovely daughter on whom I cast my eye;
She was pretty, tall, and handsome, both neat and very fair,
There's no other girl in the country with her I could compare.

I asked her if she would be willing for me to cross the plains;
She said she would be truthful until I returned again;
She said she would be faithful until death did prove unkind,
So we kissed, shook hands, and parted, and I left my girl behind.

I left the State of Texas, for Arizona I was bound;
I landed in Tombstone City, I viewed the place all round.
Money and work were plentiful and the cowboys they were kind
But the only thought of my heart was the girl I left behind.

One day as I was riding across the public square
The mail-coach came in and I met the driver there;

The Rambling Cowboy

He handed me a letter which gave me to understand
That the girl I left in Texas had married another
man.

I turned myself all round and about not knowing
what to do,
But I read on down some further and it proved the
words were true.
Hard work I have laid over, it's gambling I have
designed.
I'll ramble this wide world over for the girl I left
behind.

Come all you reckless and rambling boys who have
listened to this song,
If it hasn't done you any good, it hasn't done you
any wrong;
But when you court a pretty girl, just marry her
while you can,
For if you go across the plains she'll marry another
man.

THE COWBOY AT CHURCH

SOME time ago,— two weeks or more
    If I remember well,—
I found myself in town and thought
I'd knock around a spell,
When all at once I heard the bell,—
I didn't know 'twas Sunday,—
For on the plains we scarcely know
A Sunday from a Monday,—

A-calling all the people
From the highways and the hedges
And all the reckless throng
That tread ruin's ragged edges,
To come and hear the pastor tell
Salvation's touching story,
And how the new road misses hell
And leads you straight to glory.

I started by the chapel door,
But something urged me in,
And told me not to spend God's day
In revelry and sin.
I don't go much on sentiment,
But tears came in my eyes.
It seemed just like my mother's voice
Was speaking from the skies.

The Cowboy at Church

I thought how often she had gone
With little Sis and me
To church, when I was but a lad
Way back in Tennessee.
It never once occurred to me
About not being dressed
In Sunday rig, but carelessly
I went in with the rest.

You should have seen the smiles and shrugs
As I went walking in,
As though they thought my leggins
Worse than any kind of sin;
Although the honest parson,
In his vestry garb arrayed
Was dressed the same as I was,—
In the trappings of his trade.

The good man prayed for all the world
And all its motley crew,
For pagan, Hindoo, sinners, Turk,
And unbelieving Jew,—
Though the congregation doubtless thought
That the cowboys as a race
Were a kind of moral outlaw
With no good claim to grace.

Is it very strange that cowboys are
A rough and reckless crew
When their garb forbids their doing right
As Christian people do?

247

The Cowboy at Church

That they frequent scenes of revelry
Where death is bought and sold,
Where at least they get a welcome
Though it's prompted by their gold?

Stranger, did it ever strike you,
When the winter days are gone
And the mortal grass is springing up
To meet the judgment sun,
And we 'tend mighty round-ups
Where, according to the Word,
The angel cowboy of the Lord
Will cut the human herd,—

That a heap of stock that's lowing now
Around the Master's pen
And feeding at his fodder stack
Will have the brand picked then?
And brands that when the hair was long
Looked like the letter C,
Will prove to be the devil's,
And the brand the letter D;

While many a long-horned coaster,—
I mean, just so to speak,—
That hasn't had the advantage
Of the range and gospel creek
Will get to crop the grasses
In the pasture of the Lord
If the letter C showed up
Beneath the devil's checker board.

THE U. S. A. RECRUIT

NOW list to my song, it will not take me long,
  And in some things with me you'll agree;
A young man so green came in from Moline,
And enlisted a soldier to be.
He had lots of pluck, on himself he was stuck,
In his Government straights he looked " boss,"
And he chewed enough beans for a hoss.

  He was a rookey, so flukey,
  He was a jim dandy you all will agree,
  He said without fear, " Before I'm a year
  In the Army, great changes you'll see."
  He was a stone thrower, a foam blower,
  He was a Loo Loo you bet,
  He stood on his head and these words gently said,
" I'll be second George Washington yet."

At his post he did land, they took him in hand,
The old bucks they all gathered 'round,
Saying " Give us your fist; where did you enlist?
You'll take on again I'll be bound;
I've a blanket to sell, it will fit you quite well,
I'll sell you the whole or a piece.
I've a dress coat to trade, or a helmet unmade,
It will do you for kitchen police."

249

The U. S. A. Recruit

Then the top said, " My Son, here is a gun,
Just heel ball that musket up bright.
In a few days or more you'll be rolling in gore,
A-chasing wild Goo Goos to flight.
There'll be fighting, you see, and blood flowing free,
We'll send you right on to the front;
And never you fear, if you're wounded, my dear,
You'll be pensioned eight dollars per month."

He was worried so bad, he blew in all he had;
He went on a drunk with goodwill.
And the top did report, " One private short."
When he showed up he went to the mill.
The proceedings we find were a ten dollar blind,
Ten dollars less to blow foam.
This was long years ago, and this rookey you know
Is now in the old soldiers' home.

THE COWGIRL

MY love is a rider and broncos he breaks,
    But he's given up riding and all for my sake;
For he found him a horse and it suited him so
He vowed he'd ne'er ride any other bronco.

My love has a gun, and that gun he can use,
But he's quit his gun fighting as well as his booze;
And he's sold him his saddle, his spurs, and his rope,
And there's no more cow punching, and that's what I
    hope.

My love has a gun that has gone to the bad,
Which makes poor old Jimmy feel pretty damn sad;
For the gun it shoots high and the gun it shoots low,
And it wobbles about like a bucking bronco.

The cook is an unfortunate son of a gun;
He has to be up e'er the rise of the sun;
His language is awful, his curses are deep,—
He is like cascarets, for he works while you sleep.

THE SHANTY BOY

I AM a jolly shanty boy,
  As you will soon discover.
To all the dodges I am fly,
A hustling pine woods rover.
A peavy hook it is my pride,
An ax I well can handle;
To fell a tree or punch a bull
Get rattling Danny Randall.

Bung yer eye: bung yer eye.

I love a girl in Saginaw;
She lives with her mother;
I defy all Michigan
To find such another.
She's tall and fat, her hair is red,
Her face is plump and pretty,
She's my daisy, Sunday-best-day girl,—
And her front name stands for Kitty.

Bung yer eye: bung yer eye.

I took her to a dance one night,
A mossback gave the bidding;
Silver Jack bossed the shebang
And Big Dan played the fiddle.

The Shanty Boy

We danced and drank, the livelong night.
With fights between the dancing —
Till Silver Jack cleaned out the ranch
And sent the mossbacks prancing.

Bung yer eye: bung yer eye.

ROOT HOG OR DIE

WHEN I was a young man I lived on the square,
    I never had any pocket change and I hardly
      thought it fair;
So out on the crosses I went to rob and to steal,
And when I met a peddler oh, how happy I did feel.

One morning, one morning, one morning in May
I seen a man a-coming, a little bit far away;
I seen a man a-coming, come riding up to me
" Come here, come here, young fellow, I'm after you
      to-day."

He taken me to the new jail, he taken me to the new
      jail,
And I had to walk right in.
There all my friends went back on me
And also my kin.

I had an old rich uncle, who lived in the West,
He heard of my misfortune, it wouldn't let him rest;
He came to see me, he paid my bills and score,—
I have been a bad boy, I'll do so no more.

There's Minnie and Alice and Lucy likewise,
They heard of my misfortune brought tears to their
      eyes.

Root Hog or Die

I've told 'em my condition, I've told it o'er and o'er;
So I've been a bad boy, I'll do so no more.

I will go to East Texas to marry me a wife,
And try to maintain her the balance of my life;
I'll try to maintain; I'll lay it up in store
I've been a bad boy, I'll do so no more.

Young man, you robber, you had better take it fair,
Leave off your marshal killing and live on the square;
Should you meet the marshal, just pass him by;
And travel on the muscular, for it's root hog or die.

When I drew my money I drew it all in cash
And off to see my Susan, you bet I cut a dash;
I spent my money freely and went it on a bum,
And I love the pretty women and am bound to have
    my fun.

I used to sport a white hat, a horse and buggy fine,
Courted a pretty girl and always called her mine;
But all my courtships proved to be in vain,
For they sent me down to Huntsville to wear the
    ball and chain.

Along came my true love, about twelve o'clock,
Saying, " Henry, O Henry, what sentence have you
    got ? "
The jury found me guilty, the judge would allow no
    stay,
So they sent me down to Huntsville to wear my life
    away.

Root Hog or Die

When I was a young man I lived up-on the square,

I nev-er had a-ny pock-et change and I

hard-ly thought it fair, But out up-on the highway I

Root Hog or Die—*Concluded*

went to rob and to steal, And when I met a

ped - dler, Oh, how hap - py I did feel.

SWEET BETSY FROM PIKE

"A California Immigrant Song of the Fifties"

OH, don't you remember sweet Betsy from Pike
Who crossed the big mountains with her lover
Ike,
And two yoke of cattle, a large yellow dog,
A tall, shanghai rooster, and one spotted dog?
Saying, good-bye, Pike County,
Farewell for a while;
We'll come back again
When we've panned out our pile.

One evening quite early they camped on the Platte,
'Twas near by the road on a green shady flat;
Where Betsy, quite tired, lay down to repose,
While with wonder Ike gazed on his Pike County
rose.

They soon reached the desert, where Betsy gave out,
And down in the sand she lay rolling about;
While Ike in great terror looked on in surprise,
Saying "Betsy, get up, you'll get sand in your eyes."
Saying, good-bye, Pike County,
Farewell for a while;
I'd go back to-night
If it was but a mile.

Sweet Betsy from Pike

Sweet Betsy got up in a great deal of pain
And declared she'd go back to Pike County again;
Then Ike heaved a sigh and they fondly embraced,
And she traveled along with his arm around her
    waist.

The wagon tipped over with a terrible crash,
And out on the prairie rolled all sorts of trash;
A few little baby clothes done up with care
Looked rather suspicious,— though 'twas all on the
    square.

The shanghai ran off and the cattle all died,
The last piece of bacon that morning was fried;
Poor Ike got discouraged, and Betsy got mad,
The dog wagged his tail and looked wonderfully sad.

One morning they climbed up a very high hill,
And with wonder looked down into old Placerville;
Ike shouted and said, as he cast his eyes down,
" Sweet Betsy, my darling, we've got to Hangtown."

Long Ike and sweet Betsy attended a dance,
Where Ike wore a pair of his Pike County pants;
Sweet Betsy was covered with ribbons and rings.
Quoth Ike, " You're an angel, but where are your
    wings? "

Sweet Betsy from Pike

A miner said, " Betsy, will you dance with me?"
" I will that, old hoss, if you don't make too free;
But don't dance me hard.   Do you want to know
    why?
Dog on ye, I'm chock full of strong alkali."

Long Ike and sweet Betsy got married of course,
But Ike getting jealous obtained a divorce;
And Betsy, well satisfied, said with a shout,
" Good-bye, you big lummax, I'm glad you backed
    out."
        Saying, good-bye, dear Isaac,
        Farewell for a while,
        But come back in time
        To replenish my pile.

THE DISHEARTENED RANGER

COME listen to a ranger, you kind-hearted
    stranger,
This song, though a sad one, you're welcome to
    hear;
We've kept the Comanches away from your ranches,
And followed them far o'er the Texas frontier.

We're weary of scouting, of traveling, and routing
The blood-thirsty villains o'er prairie and wood;
No rest for the sinner, no breakfast or dinner,
But he lies in a supperless bed in the mud.

No corn nor potatoes, no bread nor tomatoes,
But jerked beef as dry as the sole of your shoe;
All day without drinking, all night without winking,
I'll tell you, kind stranger, this never will do.

Those great alligators, the State legislators,
Are puffing and blowing two-thirds of their time,
But windy orations about rangers and rations
Never put in our pockets one-tenth of a dime.

They do not regard us, they will not reward us,
Though hungry and haggard with holes in our coats;
But the election is coming and they will be drum-
    ming
And praising our valor to purchase our votes.

The Disheartened Ranger

For glory and payment, for vittles and raiment,
No longer we'll fight on the Texas frontier.
So guard your own ranches, and mind the Com-
anches
Or surely they'll scalp you in less than a year.

Though sore it may grieve you, the rangers must
leave you
Exposed to the arrows and knife of the foe;
So herd your own cattle and fight your own battle,
For home to the States I'm determined to go,—

Where churches have steeples and laws are more
equal,
Where houses have people and ladies are kind;
Where work is regarded and worth is rewarded;
Where pumpkins are plenty and pockets are lined.

Your wives and your daughters we have guarded
from slaughter,
Through conflicts and struggles I shudder to tell;
No more we'll defend them, to God we'll commend
them.
To the frontier of Texas we bid a farewell.

THE MELANCHOLY COWBOY

COME all you melancholy folks and listen unto
 me,
I will sing you about the cowboy whose heart's so
 light and free;
He roves all over the prairie and at night when he
 lays down
His heart's as gay as the flowers of May with his
 bed spread on the ground.

They are a little bit rough, I must confess, the most
 of them at least;
But as long as you do not cross their trail, you can
 live with them in peace.
But if you do, they're sure to rule, the day you come
 to their land,
For they'll follow you up and shoot it out, they'll do
 it man to man.

You can go to a cowboy hungry, go to him wet or
 dry,
And ask him for a few dollars in change and he will
 not deny;
He will pull out his pocket-book and hand you out
 a note,—
Oh, they are the fellows to strike, boys, whenever
 you are broke.

You can go to their ranches and often stay for weeks,
And when you go to leave, boys, they'll never charge
    you a cent;
But when they go to town, boys, you bet their money
    is spent.
They walk right up, they take their drinks and they
    pay for every one.
They never ask your pardon, boys, for a thing that
    they have done.

They go to the ball-room, and swing the pretty girls
    around;
They ride their bucking broncos, and wear their
    broad-brimmed hats;
Their California saddles, their pants below their
    boots,
You can hear their spurs go jing-a-ling, or perhaps
    somebody shoots.

Come all you soft and tenderfeet, if you want to
    have some fun,
Come go among the cowboys and they'll show you
    how it's done;
But take the kind advice of me as I gave it to you
    before,
For if you don't, they'll order you off with an old
    Colt's forty-four.

BOB STANFORD

BOB Stanford, he's a Texas boy,
  He lives down on the flat;
His trade is running a well-drill,
But he's none the worse for that.

He is neither rich nor handsome,
But, unlike the city dude,
His manners they are pleasant
Instead of flip and rude.

His people live in Texas,
That is his native home,
But like many other Western lads
He drifted off from home.

He came out to New Mexico
A fortune for to make,
He punched the bottom out of the earth
And never made a stake.

So he came to Arizona
And again set up his drill
To punch a hole for water,
And he's punching at it still.

He says he is determined
To make the business stick

Bob Stanford

Or spend that derned old well machine
And all he can get on tick.

I hope he is successful
And I'll help him if I can,
For I admire pluck and ambition
In an honest working man.

So keep on going down,
Punch the bottom out, or try,
There is nothing in a hole in the ground
That continues being dry.

CHARLIE RUTLAGE

ANOTHER good cow-puncher has gone to meet his fate,
I hope he'll find a resting place within the golden gate.
Another place is vacant on the ranch of the X I T,
'Twill be hard to find another that's liked as well as he.

The first that died was Kid White, a man both tough and brave,
While Charlie Rutlage makes the third to be sent to his grave,
Caused by a cow-horse falling while running after stock;
'Twas on the spring round-up,— a place where death men mock.

He went forward one morning on a circle through the hills,
He was gay and full of glee, and free from earthly ills;
But when it came to finish up the work on which he went,
Nothing came back from him; for his time on earth was spent.

'Twas as he rode the round-up, an X I T turned back
    to the herd;
Poor Charlie shoved him in again, his cutting horse
    he spurred;
Another turned; at that moment his horse the crea-
    ture spied
And turned and fell with him, and beneath, poor
    Charlie died.

His relations in Texas his face never more will see,
But I hope he will meet his loved ones beyond in
    eternity.
I hope he will meet his parents, will meet them face
    to face,
And that they will grasp him by the right hand at
    the shining throne of grace.

THE RANGE RIDERS

COME all you range riders and listen to me,
  I will relate you a story of the saddest de-
      gree,
I will relate you a story of the deepest distress,—
I love my poor Lulu, boys, of all girls the best.

When you are out riding, boys, upon the highway,
Meet a fair damsel, a lady so gay,
With her red, rosy cheeks and her sparkling dark
      eyes,
Just think of my Lulu, boys, and your bosoms will
      rise.

While you live single, boys, you are just in your
      prime;
You have no wife to scold, you have nothing to
      bother your minds;
You can roam this world over and do just as you
      will,
Hug and kiss the pretty girls and be your own still.

But when you get married, boys, you are done with
      this life,
You have sold your sweet comfort for to gain you
      a wife;

Your wife she will scold you, and the children will
    cry,
It will make those fair faces look withered and dry.

You can scarcely step aside, boys, to speak to a
    friend
But your wife is at your elbow saying what do you
    mean.
With her nose turned upon you it will look like sad
    news,—
I advise you by experience that life to refuse.

Come fill up your bottles, boys, drink Bourbon
    around;
Here is luck to the single wherever they are found.
Here is luck to the single and I wish them success,
Likewise to the married ones, I wish them no less.

I have one more request to make, boys, before we
    part.
Never place your affection on a charming sweet-
    heart.
She is dancing before you your affections to gain;
Just turn your back on them with scorn and disdain.

HER WHITE BOSOM BARE

THE sun had gone down
    O'er the hills of the west,
And the last beams had faded
O'er the mossy hill's crest,
O'er the beauties of nature
And the charms of the fair,
And Amanda was bound
With her white bosom bare.

At the foot of the mountain
Amanda did sigh
At the hoot of an owl
Or the catamount's cry;
Or the howl of some wolf
In its low, granite cell,
Or the crash of some large
Forest tree as it fell.

Amanda was there
All friendless and forlorn
With her face bathed in blood
And her garments all torn.
The sunlight had faded
O'er the hills of the green,
And fierce was the look
Of the wild, savage scene.

For it was out in the forest
Where the wild game springs,
Where low in the branches
The rude hammock swings;
The campfire was kindled,
Well fanned by the breeze,
And the light of the campfire
Shone round on the trees.

The campfire was kindled,
Well fanned by the breeze,
And the light of the fire
Shone round on the trees;
And grim stood the circle
Of the warrior throng,
Impatient to join
In the war-dance and song.

The campfire was kindled,
Each warrior was there,
And Amanda was bound
With her white bosom bare.
She counted the vengeance
In the face of her foes
And sighed for the moment
When her sufferings might close.

Young Albon, he gazed
On the face of the fair
While her dark hazel eyes

Were uplifted in prayer;
And her dark waving tresses
In ringlets did flow
Which hid from the gazer
A bosom of snow.

Then young Albon, the chief
Of the warriors, drew near,
With an eye like an eagle
And a step like a deer.
" Forbear," cried he,
" Your torture forbear;
This maiden shall live.
By my wampum I swear.

" It is for this maiden's freedom
That I do crave;
Give a sigh for her suffering
Or a tear for her grave.
If there is a victim
To be burned at that tree,
Young Albon, your leader,
That victim shall be."

Then quick to the arms
Of Amanda he rushed;
The rebel was dead,
And the tumult was hushed;
And grim stood the circle
Of warriors around

273

While the cords of Amanda
Young Albon unbound.

So it was early next morning
The red, white, and blue
Went gliding o'er the waters
In a small birch canoe;
Just like the white swan
That glides o'er the tide,
Young Albon and Amanda
O'er the waters did ride.

O'er the blue, bubbling water,
Neath the evergreen trees,
Young Albon and Amanda
Did ride at their ease;
And great was the joy
When she stepped on the shore
To embrace her dear father
And mother once more.

Young Albon, he stood
And enjoyed their embrace,
With a sigh in his heart
And a tear on his face;
And all that he asked
Was kindness and food
From the parents of Amanda
To the chief of the woods.

Her White Bosom Bare

Young Amanda is home now,
As you all know,
Enjoying the friends
Of her own native shore;
Nevermore will she roam
O'er the hills or the plains;
She praises the chief
That loosened her chains.

JUAN MURRAY

MY name is Juan Murray, and hard for my fate,
   I was born and raised in Texas, that good
      old lone star state.
I have been to many a round-up, boys, have worked
      on the trail,
Have stood many a long old guard through the rain,
      yes, sleet, and hail;
I have rode the Texas broncos that pitched from
      morning till noon,
And have seen many a storm, boys, between sunrise,
      yes, and noon.

I am a jolly cowboy and have roamed all over the
      West,
And among the bronco riders I rank among the best.
But when I left old Midland, with voice right then I
      spoke,—
" I never will see you again until the day I croak."

But since I left old Texas so many sights I have saw
A-traveling from my native state way out to
      Mexico,—
I am looking all around me and cannot help but
      smile
To see my nearest neighbors all in the Mexican
      style.

Juan Murray

I left my home in Texas to dodge the ball and chain.
In the State of Sonora I will forever remain.
Farewell to my mother, my friends that are so dear,
I would like to see you all again, my lonesome heart
    to cheer.

I have a word to speak, boys, only another to say,—
Don't never be a cow-thief, don't never ride a stray;
Be careful of your line, boys, and keep it on your
    tree,—
Just suit yourself about it, for it is nothing to me.

But if you start to rustling you will come to some
    sad fate,
You will have to go to prison and work for the state.
Don't think that I am lying and trying to tell a joke,
For the writer has experienced just every word he's
    spoke.

It is better to be honest and let other's stock alone
Than to leave your native country and seek a Mex-
    ican home.
For if you start to rustling you will surely come to
    see
The State of Sonora,— be an outcast just like me.

GREER COUNTY

TOM HIGHT is my name, an old bachelor I am,
You'll find me out West in the country of
fame,
You'll find me out West on an elegant plain,
And starving to death on my government claim.

Hurrah for Greer County!
The land of the free,
The land of the bed-bug,
Grass-hopper and flea;
I'll sing of its praises
And tell of its fame,
While starving to death
On my government claim.

My house is built of natural sod,
Its walls are erected according to hod;
Its roof has no pitch but is level and plain,
I always get wet if it happens to rain.

How happy am I on my government claim,
I've nothing to lose, and nothing to gain;
I've nothing to eat, I've nothing to wear,—
From nothing to nothing is the hardest fare.

How happy am I when I crawl into bed,—
A rattlesnake hisses a tune at my head,

Greer County

A gay little centipede, all without fear,
Crawls over my pillow and into my ear.

Now all you claim holders, I hope you will stay
And chew your hard tack till you're toothless and
    gray;
But for myself, I'll no longer remain
To starve like a dog on my government claim.

My clothes are all ragged as my language is rough,
My bread is corn dodgers, both solid and tough;
But yet I am happy, and live at my ease
On sorghum molasses, bacon, and cheese.

Good-bye to Greer County where blizzards arise,
Where the sun never sinks and a flea never dies,
And the wind never ceases but always remains
Till it starves us all out on our government claims.

Farewell to Greer County, farewell to the West,
I'll travel back East to the girl I love best,
I'll travel back to Texas and marry me a wife,
And quit corn bread for the rest of my life.

ROSIN THE BOW

I LIVE for the good of my nation
　　And my sons are all growing low,
But I hope that my next generation
Will resemble Old Rosin the Bow.

I have traveled this wide world all over,
And now to another I'll go,
For I know that good quarters are waiting
To welcome Old Rosin the Bow.

The gay round of delights I have traveled,
Nor will I behind leave a woe,
For while my companions are jovial
They'll drink to Old Rosin the Bow.

This life now is drawn to a closing,
All will at last be so,
Then we'll take a full bumper at parting
To the name of Old Rosin the Bow.

When I am laid out on the counter,
And the people all anxious to know,
Just raise up the lid of the coffin
And look at Old Rosin the Bow.

And when through the streets my friends bear me,
And the ladies are filled with deep woe,

Rosin the Bow

They'll come to the doors and the windows
And sigh for Old Rosin the Bow.

Then get some fine, jovial fellows,
And let them all staggering go;
Then dig a deep hole in the meadow
And in it toss Rosin the Bow.

Then get a couple of dornicks,
Place one at my head and my toe,
And do not forget to scratch on them,
" Here lies Old Rosin the Bow."

Then let those same jovial fellows
Surround my lone grave in a row,
While they drink from my favorite bottle
The health of Old Rosin the Bow.

THE GREAT ROUND-UP

WHEN I think of the last great round-up
    On the eve of eternity's dawn,
I think of the past of the cowboys
Who have been with us here and are gone.
And I wonder if any will greet me
On the sands of the evergreen shore
With a hearty, " God bless you, old fellow,"
That I've met with so often before.

I think of the big-hearted fellows
Who will divide with you blanket and bread,
With a piece of stray beef well roasted,
And charge for it never a red.
I often look upward and wonder
If the green fields will seem half so fair,
If any the wrong trail have taken
And fail to " be in " over there.

For the trail that leads down to perdition
Is paved all the way with good deeds,
But in the great round-up of ages,
Dear boys, this won't answer your needs.
But the way to the green pastures, though narrow,
Leads straight to the home in the sky,
And Jesus will give you the passports
To the land of the sweet by and by.

The Great Round-Up

For the Savior has taken the contract
To deliver all those who believe,
At the headquarters ranch of his Father,
In the great range where none can deceive.
The Inspector will stand at the gateway
And the herd, one by one, will go by,—
The round-up by the angels in judgment
Must pass 'neath his all-seeing eye.

No maverick or slick will be tallied
In the great book of life in his home,
For he knows all the brands and the earmarks
That down through the ages have come.
But, along with the tailings and sleepers,
The strays must turn from the gate;
No road brand to gain them admission,
But the awful sad cry " too late."

Yet I trust in the last great round-up
When the rider shall cut the big herd,
That the cowboys shall be represented
In the earmark and brand of the Lord,
To be shipped to the bright, mystic regions
Over there in green pastures to lie,
And led by the crystal still waters
In that home of the sweet by and by.

THE JOLLY COWBOY

MY lover, he is a cowboy, he's brave and kind
and true,
He rides a Spanish pony, he throws a lasso, too;
And when he comes to see me our vows we do redeem,
He throws his arms around me and thus begins to
sing:

" Ho, I'm a jolly cowboy, from Texas now I hail,
Give me my quirt and pony, I'm ready for the
trail;
I love the rolling prairies, they're free from
care and strife,
Behind a herd of longhorns I'll journey all my
life.

" When early dawn is breaking and we are far away,
We fall into our saddles, we round-up all the day;
We rope, we brand, we ear-mark, I tell you we are
smart,
And when the herd is ready, for Kansas then we
start.

" Oh, I am a Texas cowboy, lighthearted, brave, and
free,
To roam the wide, wide prairie, 'tis always joy to
me.

The Jolly Cowboy

My trusty little pony is my companion true,
O'er creeks and hills and rivers he's sure to pull me
    through.

"When threatening clouds do gather and herded
    lightnings flash,
And heavy rain drops splatter, and rolling thunders
    crash;
What keeps the herd from running, stampeding far
    and wide?
The cowboy's long, low whistle and singing by their
    side.

"When in Kansas City, our boss he pays us up,
We loaf around the city and take a parting cup;
We bid farewell to city life, from noisy crowds we
    come,
And back to dear old Texas, the cowboy's native
    home."

Oh, he is coming back to marry the only girl he
    loves,
He says I am his darling, I am his own true love;
Some day we two will marry and then no more he'll
    roam,
But settle down with Mary in a cozy little home.

"Ho, I'm a jolly cowboy, from Texas now I hail,
    Give me my bond to Mary, I'll quit the Lone
    Star trail.

The Jolly Cowboy

I love the rolling prairies, they're free from
   care and strife,
But I'll quit the herd of longhorns for the sake
   of my little wife."

The Texas Cowboy

Mrs. Robert Thomson

I am a Tex - as Cowboy, Light-hearted, gay and free,

To roam the wide, wide prairie, Is always joy to me;

My trust-y lit - tle po - ny Is my com-pan-ion true;

The Texas Cowboy—*Continued*

O'er plain, thro' woods and river, He's sure to " pull me thro."

CHORUS

Allegro

I am a jol - ly cow - boy, From Tex-as now I hail,

Give me my "quirt" and po - ny, I'm read - y for the "trail;"

I love the roll-ing prairie, We're free from care and strife,

Be-hind a herd of "long-horns" I'll journey all my life.

THE CONVICT

WHEN slumbering in my convict cell my childhood days I see,
When I was mother's little child and knelt at
mother's knee.
There my life was peace, I know, I knew no sorrow
or pain.
Mother dear never did think, I know, I would wear
a felon's chain.

Clink, clink, clink, clink, clink,
Ah, don't you hear the clinking of my chain?
Clink, clink, clink, clink, clink,
Ah, don't you hear the clinking of my chain?

When I had grown to manhood and evil paths I
trod,
I learned to scorn my fellow-man and even curse my
God;
And in the evil course I ran for a great length of
time
Till at last I ran too long and was condemned for a
felon's crime.

My prison life will soon be o'er, my life will soon be
gone,—

May the angels waft it heavenward to a bright and
    happy home.
I'll be at rest, sweet, sweet rest, there is rest in the
    heavenly home;
I'll be at rest, sweet, sweet rest, there is rest in the
    heavenly home.

    Clink, clink, clink, clink, clink,
    Ah, don't you hear the clinking of my chain?
    Clink, clink, clink, clink, clink,
    Ah, don't you hear the clinking of my chain?

JACK O' DIAMONDS

O MOLLIE, O Mollie, it is for your sake alone
    That I leave my old parents, my house and
       my home,
That I leave my old parents, you caused me to
    roam,—
I am a rabble soldier and Dixie is my home.

Jack o' diamonds, Jack o' diamonds,
I know you of old,
You've robbed my poor pockets
Of silver and gold.
Whiskey, you villain,
You've been my downfall,
You've kicked me, you've cuffed me,
But I love you for all.

My foot's in my stirrup, my bridle's in my hand,
I'm going to leave sweet Mollie, the fairest in the
    land.
Her parents don't like me, they say I'm too poor,
They say I'm unworthy to enter her door.

They say I drink whiskey; my money is my own,
And them that don't like me can leave me alone.
I'll eat when I'm hungry, I'll drink when I'm dry,
And when I get thirsty I'll lay down and cry.

It's beefsteak when I'm hungry,
And whiskey when I'm dry,
Greenbacks when I'm hard up,
And heaven when I die.
Rye whiskey, rye whiskey,
Rye whiskey I cry,
If I don't get rye whiskey,
I surely will die.
> O Baby, O Baby, I've told you before,
> Do make me a pallet, I'll lie on the floor.

I will build me a big castle on yonder mountain high,
Where my true love can see me when she comes riding by,
Where my true love can see me and help me to mourn,—
I am a rabble soldier and Dixie is my home.

I'll get up in my saddle, my quirt I'll take in hand,
I'll think of you, Mollie, when in some far distant land,
I'll think of you, Mollie, you caused me to roam,—
I am a rabble soldier and Dixie is my home.

If the ocean was whiskey,
And I was a duck,
I'd dive to the bottom
To get one sweet sup;
But the ocean ain't whiskey,
And I ain't a duck,

Jack o' Diamonds

So I'll play Jack o' diamonds
And then we'll get drunk.
 O Baby, O Baby, I've told you before,
 Do make me a pallet, I'll lie on the floor.

I've rambled and trambled this wide world around,
But it's for the rabble army, dear Mollie, I'm bound,
It is to the rabble army, dear Mollie, I roam,—
I am a rabble soldier and Dixie is my home.

I have rambled and gambled all my money away,
But it's with the rabble army, O Mollie, I must stay,
It is with the rabble army, O Mollie I must roam,—
I am a rabble soldier and Dixie is my home.

 Jack o' diamonds, Jack o' diamonds,
 I know you of old,
 You've robbed my poor pockets
 Of silver and gold.
 Rye whiskey, rye whiskey,
 Rye whiskey I cry,
 If you don't give me rye whiskey
 I'll lie down and die.
  O Baby, O Baby, I've told you before,
  Do make me a pallet, I'll lie on the floor.

Jack o' Diamonds

O Mol - lie, O Mol - lie, It's for your sake a - lone

That I leave my old pa - rents, my house and my home;

That I leave my old pa - rents, you caused me to roam—

Jack o' Diamonds—*Concluded*

I am a rab-ble sol-dier, and Dix-ie is my home.

Repeat from first for Refrain

THE COWBOY'S MEDITATION

A T midnight when the cattle are sleeping
On my saddle I pillow my head,
And up at the heavens lie peeping
From out of my cold, grassy bed,—
Often and often I wondered
At night when lying alone
If every bright star up yonder
Is a big peopled world like our own.

Are they worlds with their ranges and ranches?
Do they ring with rough rider refrains?
Do the cowboys scrap there with Comanches
And other Red Men of the plains?
Are the hills covered over with cattle
In those mystic worlds far, far away?
Do the ranch-houses ring with the prattle
Of sweet little children at play?

At night in the bright stars up yonder
Do the cowboys lie down to their rest?
Do they gaze at this old world and wonder
If rough riders dash over its breast?
Do they list to the wolves in the canyons?
Do they watch the night owl in its flight,
With their horse their only companion
While guarding the herd through the night?

The Cowboy's Meditation

Sometimes when a bright star is twinkling
Like a diamond set in the sky,
I find myself lying and thinking,
It may be God's heaven is nigh.
I wonder if there I shall meet her,
My mother whom God took away;
If in the star-heavens I'll greet her
At the round-up that's on the last day.

In the east the great daylight is breaking
And into my saddle I spring;
The cattle from sleep are awakening,
The heaven-thoughts from me take wing,
The eyes of my bronco are flashing,
Impatient he pulls at the reins,
And off round the herd I go dashing,
A reckless cowboy of the plains.

BILLY VENERO

BILLY VENERO heard them say,
  In an Arizona town one day,
That a band of Apache Indians were upon the trail
    of death;
Heard them tell of murder done,
Three men killed at Rocky Run,
"They're in danger at the cow-ranch," said Venero,
    under breath.

Cow-Ranch, forty miles away,
Was a little place that lay
In a deep and shady valley of the mighty wilderness;
Half a score of homes were there,
And in one a maiden fair
Held the heart of Billy Venero, Billy Venero's little
    Bess.

So no wonder he grew pale
When he heard the cowboy's tale
Of the men that he'd seen murdered the day before
    at Rocky Run.
"Sure as there's a God above,
I will save the girl I love;
By my love for little Bessie I will see that something's
    done."

Not a moment he delayed
When his brave resolve was made.
" Why man," his comrades told him when they heard
    of his daring plan,
" You are riding straight to death."
But he answered, " Save your breath;
I may never reach the cow-ranch but I'll do the best
    I can."

As he crossed the alkali
All his thoughts flew on ahead
To the little band at cow-ranch thinking not of
    danger near;
With his quirt's unceasing whirl
And the jingle of his spurs
Little brown Chapo bore the cowboy o'er the far
    away frontier.

Lower and lower sank the sun;
He drew rein at Rocky Run;
" Here those men met death, my Chapo," and he
    stroked his glossy mane;
" So shall those we go to warn
Ere the coming of the morn
If we fail,— God help my Bessie," and he started
    on again.

Sharp and clear a rifle shot
Woke the echoes of the spot.

" I am wounded," cried Venero, as he swayed from
 side to side;
" While there's life there's always hope;
Slowly onward I will lope,—
If I fail to reach the cow-ranch, Bessie Lee shall know
  I tried.

" I will save her yet," he cried,
" Bessie Lee shall know I tried,"
And for her sake then he halted in the shadow of a
 hill;
From his chapareras he took
With weak hands a little book;
Tore a blank leaf from its pages saying, " This shall
 be my will."

From a limb a pen he broke,
And he dipped his pen of oak
In the warm blood that was spurting from a wound
 above his heart.
" Rouse," he wrote before too late;
" Apache warriors lie in wait.
Good-bye, Bess, God bless you darling," and he felt
 the cold tears start.

Then he made his message fast,
Love's first message and its last,
To the saddle horn he tied it and his lips were white
 with pain,
" Take this message, if not me,

Straight to little Bessie Lee;"
Then he tied himself to the saddle, and he gave his
    horse the rein.

Just at dusk a horse of brown
Wet with sweat came panting down
The little lane at the cow-ranch, stopped in front of
    Bessie's door;
But the cowboy was asleep,
And his slumbers were so deep,
Little Bess could never wake him though she tried
    for evermore.

You have heard the story told
By the young and by the old,
Away down yonder at the cow-ranch the night the
    Apaches came;
Of that sharp and bloody fight,
How the chief fell in the fight
And the panic-stricken warriors when they heard
    Venero's name.

And the heavens and earth between
Keep a little flower so green
That little Bess had planted ere they laid her by his
    side.

DOGIE SONG

THE cow-bosses are good-hearted chunks,
  Some short, some heavy, more long;
But don't matter what he looks like,
They all sing the same old song.
On the plains, in the mountains, in the valleys,
In the south where the days are long,
The bosses are different fellows;
Still they sing the same old song.

" Sift along, boys, don't ride so slow;
  Haven't got much time but a long round to go.
  Quirt him in the shoulders and rake him down the
      hip;
  I've cut you toppy mounts, boys, now pair off and
      rip.
  Bunch the herd at the old meet,
  Then beat 'em on the tail;
  Whip 'em up and down the sides
  And hit the shortest trail."

303

THE BOOZER

I'M a howler from the prairies of the West.
   If you want to die with terror, look at me.
I'm chain-lightning — if I ain't, may I be blessed.
I'm the snorter of the boundless prairie.

   He's a killer and a hater!
   He's the great annihilator!
   He's a terror of the boundless prairie.

I'm the snoozer from the upper trail!
I'm the reveler in murder and in gore!
I can bust more Pullman coaches on the rail
Than anyone who's worked the job before.

   He's a snorter and a snoozer.
   He's the great trunk line abuser.
   He's the man who puts the sleeper on the rail.

I'm the double-jawed hyena from the East.
I'm the blazing, bloody blizzard of the States.
I'm the celebrated slugger; I'm the Beast.
I can snatch a man bald-headed while he waits.

   He's a double-jawed hyena!
   He's the villain of the scena!
   He can snatch a man bald-headed while he waits.

DRINKING SONG

DRINK that rot gut, drink that rot gut,
   Drink that red eye, boys;
It don't make a damn wherever we land,
We hit her up for joy.

We've lived in the saddle and ridden trail,
Drink old Jordan, boys,
We'll go whooping and yelling, we'll all go a-
      helling;
Drink her to our joy.

Whoop-ee! drink that rot gut, drink that red nose,
Whenever you get to town;
Drink it straight and swig it mighty,
Till the world goes round and round!

A FRAGMENT

I'D rather hear a rattler rattle,
   I'd rather buck stampeding cattle,
I'd rather go to a greaser battle,
Than —
Than to —
Than to fight —
Than to fight the bloody In-ji-ans.

I'd rather eat a pan of dope,
I'd rather ride without a rope,
I'd rather from this country lope,
Than —
Than to —
Than to fight —
Than to fight the bloody In-ji-ans.

A MAN NAMED HODS

COME, all you old cowpunchers, a story I will
 tell,
And if you'll all be quiet, I sure will sing it well;
And if you boys don't like it, you sure can go to hell.

Back in the day when I was young, I knew a man
 named Hods;
He wasn't fit fer nothin' 'cep turnin' up the clods.

But he came west in fifty-three, behind a pair of
 mules,
And 'twas hard to tell between the three which was
 the biggest fools.

Up on the plains old Hods he got and there his
 trouble began.
Oh, he sure did get in trouble,— and old Hodsie
 wasn't no man.

He met a bunch of Indian bucks led by Geronimo,
And what them Indians did to him, well, shorely I
 don't know.

But they lifted off old Hodsie's skelp and left him
 out to die,
And if it hadn't been for me, he'd been in the sweet
 by and by.

A Man Named Hods

But I packed him back to Santa Fé and there I found
    his mules,
For them dad-blamed two critters had got the In-
    dians fooled.

I don't know how they done it, but they shore did
    get away,
And them two mules is livin' up to this very day.

Old Hodsie's feet got toughened up, he got to be
    a sport,
He opened up a gamblin' house and a place of low
    resort;

He got the prettiest dancing girls that ever could be
    found,—
Them girls' feet was like rubber balls and they
    never staid on the ground.

And then thar came Billy the Kid, he envied Hodsie's
    wealth,
He told old Hods to leave the town, 'twould be bet-
    ter for his health;
Old Hodsie took the hint and got, but he carried all
    his wealth.

And he went back to Noo York State with lots of
    dinero,
And now they say he's senator, but of that I shore
    don't know.

A FRAGMENT

I AM fur from my sweetheart
  And she is fur from me,
And when I'll see my sweetheart
I can't tell when 'twill be.

But I love her just the same,
No matter where I roam;
And that there girl will wait fur me
Whenever I come home.

I've roamed the Texas prairies,
I've followed the cattle trail,
I've rid a pitching pony
Till the hair came off his tail.

I've been to cowboy dances,
I've kissed the Texas girls,
But they ain't none what can compare
With my own sweetheart's curls.

THE LONE STAR TRAIL

I'M a rowdy cowboy just off the stormy plains,
My trade is girting saddles and pulling bridle
reins.
Oh, I can tip the lasso, it is with graceful ease;
I rope a streak of lightning, and ride it where I
please.
My bosses they all like me, they say I am hard to
beat;
I give them the bold standoff, you bet I have got the
cheek.
I always work for wages, my pay I get in gold;
I am bound to follow the longhorn steer until I am
too old.

Ci yi yip yip yip pe ya.

I am a Texas cowboy and I do ride the range;
My trade is cinches and saddles and ropes and bridle
reins;
With Stetson hat and jingling spurs and leather up to
the knees,
Gray backs as big as chili beans and fighting like hell
with fleas.
And if I had a little stake, I soon would married be,
But another week and I must go, the boss said so
to-day.

310

My girl must cheer up courage and choose some other
    one,
For I am bound to follow the Lone Star Trail until
    my race is run.

    Ci yi yip yip yip pe ya.

It almost breaks my heart for to have to go away,
And leave my own little darling, my sweetheart so
    far away.
But when I'm out on the Lone Star Trail often I'll
    think of thee,
Of my own dear girl, the darling one, the one I
    would like to see.
And when I get to a shipping point, I'll get on a little
    spree
To drive away the sorrow for the girl that once loved
    me.
And though red licker stirs us up we're bound to
    have our fun,
And I intend to follow the Lone Star Trail until my
    race is run.

    Ci yi yip yip yip pe ya.

I went up the Lone Star Trail in eighteen eighty-
    three;
I fell in love with a pretty miss and she in love with
    me.
"When you get to Kansas write and let me know;

And if you get in trouble, your bail I'll come and go."
When I got up in Kansas, I had a pleasant dream;
I dreamed I was down on Trinity, down on that
      pleasant stream;
I dreampt my true love right beside me, she come to
      go my bail;
I woke up broken hearted with a yearling by the
      tail.

      Ci yi yip yip yip pe ya.

In came my jailer about nine o'clock,
A bunch of keys was in his hand, my cell door to
      unlock,
Saying, " Cheer up, my prisoner, I heard some voice
      say
You're bound to hear your sentence some time
      to-day."
In came my mother about ten o'clock,
Saying, " O my loving Johnny, what sentence have
      you got ? "
" The jury found me guilty and the judge a-standin'
      by
Has sent me down to Huntsville to lock me up and
      die."

      Ci yi yip yip yip pe ya.

Down come the jailer, just about eleven o'clock,
With a bunch of keys all in his hand the cell doors
      to unlock,

Saying, " Cheer up, my prisoner, I heard the jury
    say
Just ten long years in Huntsville you're bound to go
    and stay."
Down come my sweetheart, ten dollars in her hand,
Saying, " Give this to my cowboy, 'tis all that I
    command;
O give this to my cowboy and think of olden times,
Think of the darling that he has left behind."

    Ci yi yip yip yip pe ya.

WAY DOWN IN MEXICO

O BOYS, we're goin' far to-night,
   Yeo-ho, yeo-ho!
We'll take the greasers now in hand
And drive 'em in the Rio Grande,
Way down in Mexico.

We'll hang old Santa Anna soon,
Yeo-ho, yeo-ho!
And all the greaser soldiers, too,
To the chune of Yankee Doodle Doo,
Way down in Mexico.

We'll scatter 'em like flocks of sheep,
Yeo-ho, yeo-ho!
We'll mow 'em down with rifle ball
And plant our flag right on their wall,
Way down in Mexico.

Old Rough and Ready, he's a trump,
Yeo-ho, yeo-ho!
He'll wipe old Santa Anna out
And put the greasers all to rout,
Way down in Mexico.

Then we'll march back by and by,
Yeo-ho, yeo-ho!
And kiss the gals we left to home
And never more we'll go and roam,
Way down in Mexico.

RATTLESNAKE — A RANCH HAYING
SONG

A NICE young ma-wa-wan
 Lived on a hi-wi-will;
A nice young ma-wa-wan,
For I knew him we-we-well.

 To my rattle, to my roo-rah-ree!

This nice young ma-wa-wan
Went out to mo-wo-wow
To see if he-we-we
Could make a sho-wo-wow.

 To my rattle, to my roo-rah-ree!

He scarcely mo-wo-wowed
Half round the fie-we-wield
Till up jumped — come a rattle, come a sna-wa-wake,
And bit him on the he-we-weel.

 To my rattle, to my roo-rah-ree!

He laid right dow-wo-wown
Upon the gro-wo-wound
And shut his ey-wy-wyes
And looked all aro-wo-wound.

 To my rattle, to my roo-rah-ree!

Rattlesnake — A Ranch Haying Song

" O pappy da-wa-wad,
Go tell my ga-wa-wal
That I'm a-goin' ter di-wi-wie,
For I know I sha-wa-wall.

To my rattle, to my roo-rah-ree!

" O pappy da-wa-wad,
Go spread the ne-wu-wus;
And here come Sa-wa-wall
Without her sho-woo-woos."

To my rattle, to my roo-rah-ree!

" O John, O Joh-wa-wahn,
Why did you go-wo-wo
Way down in the mea-we-we-dow
So far to mo-wo-wow?"

To my rattle, to my roo-rah-ree!

" O Sal, O Sa-wa-wall,
Why don't you kno-wo-wow
When the grass gits ri-wi-wipe,
It must be mo-wo-woed?"

To my rattle, to my roo-rah-ree!

Come all young gir-wi-wirls
And shed a tea-we-wear

Rattlesnake — A Ranch Haying Song

For this young ma-wa-wan
That died right he-we-were.

    To my rattle, to my roo-rah-ree!

Come all young me-we-wen
And warning ta-wa-wake,
And don't get bi-wi-wit
By a rattle sna-wa-wake.

    To my rattle, to my roo-rah-ree!

THE RAILROAD CORRAL

OH we're up in the morning ere breaking of day,
  The chuck wagon's busy, the flapjacks in play;
The herd is astir o'er hillside and vale,
With the night riders rounding them into the trail.
  Oh, come take up your cinches, come shake out
      your reins;
Come wake your old broncho and break for the
      plains;
  Come roust out your steers from the long chapar-
      ral,
  For the outfit is off to the railroad corral.

The sun circles upward; the steers as they plod
Are pounding to powder the hot prairie sod;
And it seems as the dust makes you dizzy and sick
That we'll never reach noon and the cool, shady
      creek.
  But tie up your kerchief and ply up your nag;
  Come dry up your grumbles and try not to lag;
  Come with your steers from the long chaparral,
  For we're far on the road to the railroad corral.

The afternoon shadows are starting to lean,
When the chuck wagon sticks in the marshy ravine;
The herd scatters farther than vision can look,

The Railroad Corral

For you can bet all true punchers will help out the
    cook.
  Come shake out your rawhide and snake it up
    fair;
  Come break your old broncho to take in his share;
  Come from your steers in the long chaparral,
  For 'tis all in the drive to the railroad corral.

But the longest of days must reach evening at last,
The hills all climbed, the creeks all past;
The tired herd droops in the yellowing light;
Let them loaf if they will, for the railroad's in sight,
  So flap up your holster and snap up your belt,
  And strap up your saddle whose lap you have felt;
  Good-bye to the steers from the long chaparral,
  For there's a town that's a trunk by the railroad
    corral.

THE SONG OF THE "METIS" TRAPPER

BY ROLETTE

HURRAH for the great white way!
　　Hurrah for the dog and sledge!
As we snow-shoe along,
　　We give them a song,
With a snap of the whip and an urgent "mush
　　　　on,"—
　　Hurrah for the great white way!　Hurrah!

Hurrah for the snow and the ice!
　　As we follow the trail,
We call to the dogs with whistle and song,
　　And reply to their talk
With only "mush on, mush on"!
　　Hurrah for the snow and the ice!　Hurrah!

Hurrah for the gun and the trap,—
　　As we follow the lines
By the rays of the mystic light
　　That flames in the north with banners so bright,
As we list to its swish, swish, swish, through the air
　　　　all night,
　　Hurrah for the gun and the trap!　Hurrah!　Hur-
　　　　rah!　Hurrah!

The Song of the "Metis" Trapper

Hurrah for the fire and cold!
  As we lie in the robes all night.
And list to the howl of the wolf;
  For we emptied the pot of the tea so hot,
And a king on his throne might envy our lot,—
  Hurrah for the fire and cold! Hurrah!

Hurrah for our black-haired girls,
  Who brave the storms of the mountain heights
And follow us on the great white way;
  For their eyes so bright light the way all right
And guide us to shelter and warmth each night.
  Hurrah for our black-haired girls! Hurrah!
    Hurrah! Hurrah!

THE CAMP FIRE HAS GONE OUT

THROUGH progress of the railroads our occu-
pation's gone;
So we will put ideas into words, our words into a
song.
First comes the cowboy, he is pointed for the west;
Of all the pioneers I claim the cowboys are the best;
You will miss him on the round-up, it's gone, his
merry shout,—
The cowboy has left the country and the campfire
has gone out.

There is the freighters, our companions, you've got
to leave this land,
Can't drag your loads for nothing through the
gumbo and the sand.
The railroads are bound to beat you when you do
your level best;
So give it up to the grangers and strike out for the
west.
Bid them all adieu and give the merry shout,—
The cowboy has left the country and the campfire has
gone out.

When I think of those good old days, my eyes with
tears do fill;

The Camp Fire Has Gone Out

When I think of the tin can by the fire and the
    cayote on the hill.
I'll tell you, boys, in those days old-timers stood a
    show,—
Our pockets full of money, not a sorrow did we
    know.
But things have changed now, we are poorly clothed
    and fed.
Our wagons are all broken and our ponies most all
    dead.
Soon we will leave this country, you'll hear the angels
    shout,
" Oh, here they come to Heaven, the campfire has
    gone out."

NIGHT-HERDING SONG

BY HARRY STEPHENS

OH, slow up, dogies, quit your roving round,
  You have wandered and tramped all over the
    ground;
Oh, graze along, dogies, and feed kinda slow,
And don't forever be on the go,—
Oh, move slow, dogies, move slow.

Hi-oo, hi-oo, oo-oo.

I have circle-herded, trail-herded, night-herded, and
    cross-herded, too,
But to keep you together, that's what I can't do;
My horse is leg weary and I'm awful tired,
But if I let you get away I'm sure to get fired,—
Bunch up, little dogies, bunch up.

Hi-oo, hi-oo, oo-oo.

O say, little dogies, when you goin' to lay down
And quit this forever siftin' around?
My limbs are weary, my seat is sore;
Oh, lay down, dogies, like you've laid before,—
Lay down, little dogies, lay down.

Hi-oo, hi-oo, oo-oo.

Night-Herding Song

Oh, lay still, dogies, since you have laid down,
Stretch away out on the big open ground;
Snore loud, little dogies, and drown the wild sound
That will all go away when the day rolls round,—
Lay still, little dogies, lay still.

Hi-oo, hi-oo, oo-oo.

TAIL PIECE

Oh, the cow-puncher loves the whistle of his rope,
As he races over the plains;
And the stage-driver loves the popper of his whip,
And the rattle of his concord chains;
And we'll all pray the Lord that we will be saved,
And we'll keep the golden rule;
But I'd rather be home with the girl I love
Than to monkey with this goddamn'd mule.

* * * * * * * * * *

THE HABIT *

I'VE beat my way wherever any winds have blown,
   I've bummed along from Portland down to San
     Antone,
From Sandy Hook to Frisco, over gulch and hill;
For once you git the habit, why, you can't keep still.

I settles down quite frequent and I says, says I,
" I'll never wander further till I comes to die."
But the wind it sorta chuckles, " Why, o' course you
     will,"
And shure enough I does it, cause I can't keep still.

I've seed a lot o' places where I'd like to stay,
But I gets a feelin' restless and I'm on my way.
I was never meant for settin' on my own door sill,
And once you git the habit, why, you can't keep still.

I've been in rich men's houses and I've been in jail,
But when it's time for leavin', I jes hits the trail;
I'm a human bird of passage, and the song I trill,
Is, " Once you git the habit, why, you can't keep
     still."

* A song current in Arizona, probably written by Berton Braley.
Cowboys and miners often take verses that please them and fit
them to music.

327

The Habit

The sun is sorta coaxin' and the road is clear
And the wind is singin' ballads that I got to hear.
It ain't no use to argue when you feel the thrill;
For once you git the habit, why, you can't keep still.

OLD PAINT *

REFRAIN:
    Goodbye, Old Paint, I'm a-leavin' Cheyenne,
Goodbye, Old Paint, I'm a-leavin' Cheyenne,—

My foot in the stirrup, my pony won't stand;
Goodbye, Old Paint, I'm a-leavin' Cheyenne.

I'm a-leavin' Cheyenne, I'm off for Montan';
Goodbye, Old Paint, I'm a-leavin' Cheyenne.

I'm a ridin' Old Paint, I'm a-leadin' old Fan;
Goodbye, Old Paint, I'm a-leavin' Cheyenne.

With my feet in the stirrups, my bridle in my hand;
Goodbye, Old Paint, I'm a-leavin' Cheyenne.

Old Paint's a good pony, he paces when he can;
Goodbye, little Annie, I'm off for Cheyenne.

Oh, hitch up your horses and feed 'em some hay,
And seat yourself by me so long as you stay.

* These verses are used in many parts of the West as a dance song. Sung to waltz music the song takes the place of "Home, Sweet Home" at the conclusion of a cowboy ball. The "fiddle" is silenced and the entire company sing as they dance.

Old Paint

My horses ain't hungry, they'll not eat your hay;
My wagon is loaded and rolling away.

My foot in my stirrup, my reins in my hand;
Good-morning, young lady, my horses won't stand.

Goodbye, Old Paint, I'm a-leavin' Cheyenne.
Goodbye, Old Paint, I'm a-leavin' Cheyenne.

DOWN SOUTH ON THE RIO GRANDE

FROM way down south on the Rio Grande,
Roll on steers for the Post Oak Sand,—
Way down south in Dixie, Oh, boys, Ho.

You'd laugh fur to see that fellow a-straddle
Of a mustang mare on a raw-hide saddle,—
Way down south in Dixie, Oh, boys, Ho.

Rich as a king, and he wouldn't be bigger
Fur a pitchin' hoss and a lame old nigger,—
Way down south in Dixie, Oh, boys, Ho.

Ole Abe kep' gettin' bigger an' bigger,
'Til he bust hisself 'bout a lame old nigger,—
Way down south in Dixie, Oh, boys, Ho.

Old Jeff swears he'll sew him together
With powder and shot instead of leather,—
Way down south in Dixie, Oh, boys, Ho.

Kin cuss an' fight an' hold or free 'em,
But I know them mavericks when I see 'em,—
Way down south in Dixie, Oh, boys, Ho.

SILVER JACK *

I WAS on the drive in eighty
　　Working under Silver Jack,
Which the same is now in Jackson
And ain't soon expected back,
And there was a fellow 'mongst us
By the name of Robert Waite;
Kind of cute and smart and tonguey
Guess he was a graduate.

He could talk on any subject
From the Bible down to Hoyle,
And his words flowed out so easy,
Just as smooth and slick as oil,
He was what they call a skeptic,
And he loved to sit and weave
Hifalutin' words together
Tellin' what he didn't believe.

One day we all were sittin' round
Smokin' nigger head tobacco
And hearing Bob expound;
Hell, he said, was all a humbug,
And he made it plain as day
That the Bible was a fable;

* A lumber jack song adopted by the cowboys.

332

And we lowed it looked that way.
Miracles and such like
Were too rank for him to stand,
And as for him they called the Savior
He was just a common man.

"You're a liar," someone shouted,
"And you've got to take it back."
Then everybody started,—
'Twas the words of Silver Jack.
And he cracked his fists together
And he stacked his duds and cried,
"'Twas in that thar religion
That my mother lived and died;
And though I haven't always
Used the Lord exactly right,
Yet when I hear a chump abuse him
He's got to eat his words or fight."

Now, this Bob he weren't no coward
And he answered bold and free:
"Stack your duds and cut your capers,
For there ain't no flies on me."
And they fit for forty minutes
And the crowd would whoop and cheer
When Jack spit up a tooth or two,
Or when Bobby lost an ear.

But at last Jack got him under
And he slugged him onct or twict,

And straightway Bob admitted
The divinity of Christ.
But Jack kept reasoning with him
Till the poor cuss gave a yell
And lowed he'd been mistaken
In his views concerning hell.

Then the fierce encounter ended
And they riz up from the ground
And someone brought a bottle out
And kindly passed it round.
And we drank to Bob's religion
In a cheerful sort o' way,
But the spread of infidelity
Was checked in camp that day.

THE COWBOY'S CHRISTMAS BALL *

WAY out in Western Texas, where the Clear
⠀⠀⠀Fork's waters flow,
Where the cattle are a-browzin' and the Spanish
⠀⠀⠀ponies grow;
Where the Northers come a-whistlin' from beyond
⠀⠀⠀the Neutral Strip;
And the prairie dogs are sneezin', as though they
⠀⠀⠀had the grip;
Where the coyotes come a-howlin' round the ranches
⠀⠀⠀after dark,
And the mockin' birds are singin' to the lovely med-
⠀⠀⠀der lark;
Where the 'possum and the badger and the rattle-
⠀⠀⠀snakes abound,
And the monstrous stars are winkin' o'er a wilder-
⠀⠀⠀ness profound;
Where lonesome, tawny prairies melt into airy
⠀⠀⠀streams,

* This poem, one of the best in Larry Chittenden's *Ranch
Verses,* published by G. P. Putnam's Sons, New York, has been set
to music by the cowboys and its phraseology slightly changed, as
this copy will show, by oral transmission. I have heard it in
New Mexico and it has been sent to me from various places,—
always as a song. None of those who sent in the song knew
that it was already in print.

While the Double Mountains slumber in heavenly
    kinds of dreams;
Where the antelope is grazin' and the lonely plov-
    ers call,—
It was there I attended the Cowboy's Christmas
    Ball.

The town was Anson City, old Jones' county seat,
Where they raised Polled Angus cattle and waving
    whiskered wheat;
Where the air is soft and bammy and dry and full
    of health,
Where the prairies is explodin' with agricultural
    wealth;
Where they print the *Texas Western,* that Hec
    McCann supplies
With news and yarns and stories, of most amazing
    size;
Where Frank Smith " pulls the badger " on know-
    ing tenderfeet,
And Democracy's triumphant and mighty hard to
    beat;
Where lives that good old hunter, John Milsap,
    from Lamar,
Who used to be the sheriff " back east in Paris,
    sah "!
'Twas there, I say, at Anson with the lovely Widder
    Wall,
That I went to that reception, the Cowboy's Christ-
    mas Ball.

The boys had left the ranches and come to town in
piles;
The ladies, kinder scatterin', had gathered in for
miles.
And yet the place was crowded, as I remember well,
'Twas gave on this occasion at the Morning Star
Hotel.
The music was a fiddle and a lively tambourine,
And a viol came imported, by the stage from Abi-
lene.
The room was togged out gorgeous — with mistle-
toe and shawls,
And the candles flickered festious, around the airy
walls.
The wimmen folks looked lovely — the boys looked
kinder treed,
Till the leader commenced yelling, " Whoa, fellers,
let's stampede,"
And the music started sighing and a-wailing through
the hall
As a kind of introduction to the Cowboy's Christ-
mas Ball.

The leader was a feller that came from Swenson's
ranch,—
They called him Windy Billy from Little Dead-
man's Branch.
His rig was kinder keerless,— big spurs and high
heeled boots;
He had the reputation that comes when fellers
shoots.

His voice was like the bugle upon the mountain
    height;

His feet were animated, and a mighty movin' sight,

When he commenced to holler, " Now fellers, shake
    your pen!

Lock horns ter all them heifers and rustle them like
    men;

Saloot yer lovely critters; neow swing and let 'em
    go;

Climb the grapevine round 'em; neow all hands do-
    ce-do!

You maverick, jine the round-up,— jes skip the
    waterfall,"

Huh! hit was getting active, the Cowboy's Christmas
    Ball.

The boys was tolerable skittish, the ladies powerful
    neat,

That old bass viol's music just got there with both
    feet!

That wailin', frisky fiddle, I never shall forget;

And Windy kept a-singin'— I think I hear him
    yet —

" Oh, X's, chase yer squirrels, and cut 'em to our
    side;

Spur Treadwell to the center, with Cross P Char-
    ley's bride,

Doc Hollis down the center, and twine the ladies'
    chain,

Van Andrews, pen the fillies in big T Diamond's
    train.

The Cowboy's Christmas Ball

All pull your freight together, neow swallow fork
and change;
Big Boston, lead the trail herd through little Pitch-
fork's range.
Purr round yer gentle pussies, neow rope and bal-
ance all!"
Huh! Hit were gettin' active — the Cowboy's
Christmas Ball.

The dust riz fast and furious; we all jes galloped
round,
Till the scenery got so giddy that T Bar Dick was
downed.
We buckled to our partners and told 'em to hold on,
Then shook our hoofs like lightning until the early
dawn.
Don't tell me 'bout cotillions, or germans. No
sir-ee!
That whirl at Anson City jes takes the cake with me.
I'm sick of lazy shufflin's, of them I've had my fill,
Give me a frontier break-down backed up by Windy
Bill.
McAllister ain't nowhere, when Windy leads the
show;
I've seen 'em both in harness and so I ought ter
know.
Oh, Bill, I shan't forget yer, and I oftentimes recall
That lively gaited sworray — the Cowboy's Christ-
mas Ball.

PINTO

I AM a vaquero by trade;
To handle my rope I'm not afraid.
I lass' an *otero* by the two horns
Throw down the biggest that ever was born.
Whoa! Whoa! Whoa! Pinto, whoa!

My name to you I will not tell;
For what's the use, you know me so well.
The girls all love me, and cry
When I leave them to join the rodero.
Whoa! Whoa! Whoa! Pinto, whoa!

I am a vaquero, and here I reside;
Show me the broncho I cannot ride.
They say old Pinto with one split ear
Is the hardest jumping broncho on the rodero.
Whoa! Whoa! Whoa! Pinto, whoa!

There strayed to our camp an iron gray colt;
The boys were all fraid him so on him I bolt.
You bet I stayed with him till cheer after cheer,—
"He's the broncho twister that's on the rodero."
Whoa! Whoa! Whoa! Pinto, whoa!

340

Pinto

My story is ended, old Pinto is dead;
I'm going down Laredo and paint the town red.
I'm going up to Laredo and set up the beer
To all the cowboys that's on the rodero.
Whoa! Whoa! Whoa! Pinto, whoa!

THE GAL I LEFT BEHIND ME

I STRUCK the trail in seventy-nine,
    The herd strung out behind me;
As I jogged along my mind ran back
For the gal I left behind me.
      That sweet little gal, that true little **gal**,
      The gal I left behind me!

If ever I get off the trail
And the Indians they don't find me,
I'll make my way straight back again
To the gal I left behind me.
      That sweet little gal, that true little **gal**,
      The gal I left behind me!

The wind did blow, the rain did flow,
The hail did fall and blind me;
I thought of that gal, that sweet little **gal**,
That gal I'd left behind me!
      That sweet little gal, that true little **gal**,
      The gal I left behind me!

She wrote ahead to the place I said,
I was always glad to find it.
She says, " I am true, when you get through
Right back here you will find me."

The Gal I Left Behind Me

That sweet little gal, that true little **gal**,
The gal I left behind me!

When we sold out I took the train,
I knew where I would find her;
When I got back we had a smack
And that was no gol-darned liar.
That sweet little gal, that true little **gal**,
The gal I left behind me!

BILLY THE KID

BILLY was a bad man
And carried a big gun,
He was always after Greasers
And kept 'em on the run.

He shot one every morning,
For to make his morning meal.
And let a white man sass him,
He was shore to feel his steel.

He kept folks in hot water,
And he stole from many a stage;
And when he was full of liquor
He was always in a rage.

But one day he met a man
Who was a whole lot badder.
And now he's dead,
And we ain't none the sadder.

THE HELL-BOUND TRAIN

A TEXAS cowboy lay down on a bar-room floor,
Having drunk so much he could drink no more;
So he fell asleep with a troubled brain
To dream that he rode on a hell-bound train.

The engine with murderous blood was damp
And was brilliantly lit with a brimstone lamp;
An imp, for fuel, was shoveling bones,
While the furnace rang with a thousand groans.

The boiler was filled with lager beer
And the devil himself was the engineer;
The passengers were a most motley crew,—
Church member, atheist, Gentile, and Jew,

Rich men in broadcloth, beggars in rags,
Handsome young ladies, and withered old hags,
Yellow and black men, red, brown, and white,
All chained together,— O God, what a sight!

While the train rushed on at an awful pace,
The sulphurous fumes scorched their hands and
      face;
Wider and wider the country grew,
As faster and faster the engine flew.

The Hell-Bound Train

Louder and louder the thunder crashed
And brighter and brighter the lightning flashed;
Hotter and hotter the air became
Till the clothes were burnt from each quivering
    frame.

And out of the distance there arose a yell,
" Ha, ha," said the devil, " we're nearing hell! "
Then oh, how the passengers all shrieked with pain
And begged the devil to stop the train.

But he capered about and danced for glee
And laughed and joked at their misery.
" My faithful friends, you have done the work
And the devil never can a payday shirk.

" You've bullied the weak, you've robbed the poor;
The starving brother you've turned from the door,
You've laid up gold where the canker rust,
And have given free vent to your beastly lust.

" You've justice scorned, and corruption sown,
And trampled the laws of nature down.
You have drunk, rioted, cheated, plundered, and
    lied,
And mocked at God in your hell-born pride.

" You have paid full fare so I'll carry you through;
For it's only right you should have your due.
Why, the laborer always expects his hire,
So I'll land you safe in the lake of fire.

"Where your flesh will waste in the flames that roar,
And my imps torment you forever more."
Then the cowboy awoke with an anguished cry,
His clothes wet with sweat and his hair standing
high.

Then he prayed as he never had prayed till that hour
To be saved from his sin and the demon's power.
And his prayers and his vows were not in vain;
For he never rode the hell-bound train.

THE OLD SCOUT'S LAMENT

COME all of you, my brother scouts,
    And listen to my song;
Come, let us sing together
Though the shadows fall so long.

Of all the old frontiersmen
That used to scour the plain
There are but very few of them
That with us yet remain.

Day after day they're dropping off,
They're going one by one;
Our clan is fast decreasing,
Our race is almost run.

There are many of our number
That never wore the blue,
But faithfully they did their part
As brave men, tried and true.

They never joined the army,
But had other work to do
In piloting the coming folks,
To help them safely through.

The Old Scout's Lament

But brothers, we are failing,
Our race is almost run;
The days of elk and buffalo
And beaver traps are gone —

Oh, the days of elk and buffalo!
It fills my heart with pain
To know these days are past and gone
To never come again.

We fought the red-skin rascals
Over valley, hill, and plain;
We fought him in the mountain top,
We fought him down again.

These fighting days are over.
The Indian yell resounds
No more along the border;
Peace sends far sweeter sounds.

But we found great joy, old comrades,
To hear and make it die;
We won bright homes for gentle ones,
And now, our West, good-bye.

THE DESERTED ADOBE

ROUND the 'dobe rank sands are thickly blowin',
   Its ridges fill the deserted field;
Yet on this claim young lives once hope were sowing
For all the years might yield;
And in strong hands the echoing hoof pursuin'
A wooden share turned up the sod,
The toiler brave drank deep the fresh air's brewin'
And sang content to God.
   The toiler brave drank deep the fresh air's brewin'
   And sang content to God.

A woman fair and sweet has smilin' striven
Through long and lonesome hours;
A blue-eyed babe, a bit of earthly heaven,
Laughed at the sun's hot towers;
A bow of promise made this desert splendid,
This 'dobe was their pride.
But what began so well, alas, has ended —,
The promise died.
   But what began so well alas soon ended —,
   The promise died.

Their plans and dreams, their cheerful labor wasted
In dry and mis-spent years;
The spring was sweet, the summer bitter tasted,

The autumn salt with tears.
Now " gyp " and sand do hide their one-time
 yearnin';
'Twas theirs; 'tis past.
God's ways are strange, we take so long in learnin',
To fail at last.

 God's ways are strange, we take so long in
  learnin',
  To fail at last.

THE COWBOY AT WORK

YOU may call the cowboy horned and think him
      hard to tame,
You may heap vile epithets upon his head;
But to know him is to like him, notwithstanding his
      hard name,
For he will divide with you his beef and bread.

If you see him on his pony as he scampers o'er the
      plain,
You would think him wild and woolly, to be sure;
But his heart is warm and tender when he sees a
      friend in need,
Though his education is but to endure.

When the storm breaks in its fury and the light-
      ning's vivid flash
Makes you thank the Lord for shelter and for bed,
Then it is he mounts his pony and away you see him
      dash,
No protection but the hat upon his head.

Such is life upon a cow ranch, and the half was never
      told;
But you never find a kinder-hearted set

Than the cattleman at home, be he either young or
    old,
He's a " daisy from away back," don't forget.

When you fail to find a pony or a cow that's gone
    a-stray,
Be that cow or pony wild or be it tame,
The cowboy, like the drummer,— and the bed-bug,
    too, they say,—
Brings him to you, for he gets there just the same.

HERE'S TO THE RANGER!

HE leaves unplowed his furrow,
  He leaves his books unread
For a life of tented freedom
By lure of danger led.
He's first in the hour of peril,
He's gayest in the dance,
Like the guardsman of old England
Or the beau sabreur of France.

He stands our faithful bulwark
Against our savage foe;
Through lonely woodland places
Our children come and go;
Our flocks and herds untended
O'er hill and valley roam,
The Ranger in the saddle
Means peace for us at home.

Behold our smiling farmsteads
Where waves the golden grain!
Beneath yon tree, earth's bosom
Was dark with crimson stain.
That bluff the death-shot echoed
Of husband, father, slain!

354

Here's to the Ranger!

God grant such sight of horror
We never see again!

The gay and hardy Ranger,
His blanket on the ground,
Lies by the blazing camp-fire
While song and tale goes round;
And if one voice is silent,
One fails to hear the jest,
They know his thoughts are absent
With her who loves him best.

Our state, her sons confess it,
That queenly, star-crowned brow,
Has darkened with the shadow
Of lawlessness ere now;
And men of evil passions
On her reproach have laid,
But that the ready Ranger
Rode promptly to her aid.

He may not win the laurel
Nor trumpet tongue of fame;
But beauty smiles upon him,
And ranchmen bless his name.
Then here's to the Texas Ranger,
Past, present and to come!
Our safety from the savage,
The guardian of our home.

MUSTER OUT THE RANGER

YES, muster them out, the valiant band
    That guards our western home.
What matter to you in your eastern land
If the raiders here should come?
No danger that you shall awake at night
To the howls of a savage band;
So muster them out, though the morning light
Find havoc on every hand.

Some dear one is sick and the horses all gone,
So we can't for a doctor send;
The outlaws were in in the light of the morn
And no Rangers here to defend.
For they've mustered them out, the brave true band,
Untiring by night and day.
The fearless scouts of this border land
Made the taxes high, they say.

Have fewer men in the capitol walls,
Fewer tongues in the war of words,
But add to the Rangers, the living wall
That keeps back the bandit hordes.
Have fewer dinners, less turtle soup,
If the taxes are too high.

Muster Out the Ranger

There are many other and better ways
To lower them if they try.

Don't waste so much of your money
Printing speeches people don't read.
If you'd only take off what's used for that
'Twould lower the tax indeed.
Don't use so much sugar and lemons;
Cold water is just as good
For a constant drink in the summer time
And better for the blood.

But leave us the Rangers to guard us still,
Nor think that they cost too dear;
For their faithful watch over vale and hill
Gives our loved ones naught to fear.

A COW CAMP ON THE RANGE

OH, the prairie dogs are screaming,
    And the birds are on the wing,
See the heel fly chase the heifer, boys!
'Tis the first class sign of spring.
The elm wood is budding,
The earth is turning green.
See the pretty things of nature
That make life a pleasant dream!

I'm just living through the winter
To enjoy the coming change,
For there is no place so homelike
As a cow camp on the range.
The boss is smiling radiant,
Radiant as the setting sun;
For he knows he's stealing glories,
For he ain't a-cussin' none.

The cook is at the chuck-box
Whistling " Heifers in the Green,"
Making baking powder biscuits, boys,
While the pot is biling beans.
The boys untie their bedding
And unroll it on the run,

A Cow Camp on the Range

For they are in a monstrous hurry
For the supper's almost done.

" Here's your bloody wolf bait,"
Cried the cook's familiar voice
As he climbed the wagon wheel
To watch the cowboys all rejoice.
Then all thoughts were turned from reverence
To a plate of beef and beans,
As we graze on beef and biscuits
Like yearlings on the range.

To the dickens with your city
Where they herd the brainless brats,
On a range so badly crowded
There ain't room to cuss the cat.
This life is not so sumptuous,
I'm not longing for a change,
For there is no place so homelike
As a cow camp on the range.

FRECKLES.   A FRAGMENT

HE was little an' peaked an' thin, an' narry a no
    account horse,—
Least that's the way you'd describe him in case that
    the beast had been lost;
But, for single and double cussedness an' for double
    fired sin,
The horse never came out o' Texas that was half-
    way knee-high to him!

The first time that ever I saw him was nineteen years
    ago last spring;
'Twas the year we had grasshoppers, that come an'
    et up everything,
That a feller rode up here one evenin' an' wanted
    to pen over night
A small bunch of horses, he said; an' I told him I
    guessed 'twas all right.

Well, the feller was busted, the horses was thin, an'
    the grass round here kind of good,
An' he said if I'd let him hold here a few days he'd
    settle with me when he could.

Freckles. *A Fragment*

So I told him all right, turn them loose down the
    draw, that the latch string was always untied,
He was welcome to stop a few days if he wished
    and rest from his weary ride.

Well, the cuss stayed around for two or three weeks,
    till at last he was ready to go;
And that cuss out yonder bein' too poor to move, he
    gimme,— the cuss had no dough.
Well, at first the darn brute was as wild as a deer,
    an' would snort when he came to the branch,
An' it took two cow punchers, on good horses, too,
    to handle him here at the ranch.

Well, the winter came on an' the range it got hard,
    an' my mustang commenced to get thin,
So I fed him some an' rode him around, an' found
    out old Freckles was game.
For that was what the other cuss called him,— just
    Freckles, no more or no less,—
His color,— couldn't describe it,— something like a
    paint shop in distress.

Them was Indian times, young feller, that I am tell-
    ing about;
An' oft's the time I've seen the red man fight an'
    put the boys to rout.
A good horse in them days, young feller, would save
    your life,—
One that in any race could hold the pace when the
    red-skin bands were rife.

*   *   *   *   *   *   *

WHOSE OLD COW?

'TWAS the end of round-up, the last day of
June,
Or maybe July, I don't remember,
Or it might have been August, 'twas some time ago,
Or perhaps 'twas the first of September.

Anyhow, 'twas the round-up we had at Mayou
On the Lightning Rod's range, near Cayo;
There were some twenty wagons, more or less,
camped about
On the temporal in the cañon.

First night we'd no cattle, so we only stood guard
On the horses, somewhere near two hundred head;
So we side-lined and hoppled, we belled and we
staked,
Loosed our hot-rolls and fell into bed.

Next morning 'bout day break we started our work,
Our horses, like 'possums, felt fine.
Each one " tendin' knittin'," none tryin' to shirk!
So the round-up got on in good time.

362

Well, we worked for a week till the country was
    clean
And the bosses said, " Now, boys, we'll stay here.
We'll carve and we'll trim 'em and start out a herd
Up the east trail from old Abilene."

Next morning all on herd, and but two with the cut,
And the boss on Piute, carving fine,
Till he rode down his horse and had to pull out,
And a new man went in to clean up.

Well, after each outfit had worked on the band
There was only three head of them left;
When Nig Add from L F D outfit rode in,—
A dictionary on earmarks and brands.

He cut the two head out, told where they belonged;
But when the last cow stood there alone
Add's eyes bulged so he didn't know just what to say,
'Ceptin', " Boss, dere's something here monstrous
    wrong!

" White folks smarter'n Add, and maybe I'se wrong;
But here's six months' wages dat I'll give
If anyone'll tell me when I reads dis mark
To who dis longhorned cow belong!

" Overslope in right ear an' de underbill,
Lef' ear swaller fork an' de undercrop,
Hole punched in center, an' de jinglebob
Under half crop, an' de slash an' split.

" She's got O Block an' Lightnin' Rod,
Nine Forty-Six an' A Bar Eleven,
T Terrapin an' Ninety-Seven,
Rafter Cross an' de Double Prod.

" Half circle A an' Diamond D,
Four Cross L and Three P Z,
B W I bar, X V V,
Bar N cross an' A L C.

" So, if none o' you punchers claims dis cow,
Mr. Stock 'Sociation needn't git 'larmed;
For one more brand more or less won't do no harm,
So old Nigger Add'l just brand her now."

OLD TIME COWBOY

COME all you melancholy folks wherever you
    may be,
I'll sing you about the cowboy whose life is light and
    free.
He roams about the prairie, and, at night when he
    lies down,
His heart is as gay as the flowers in May in his bed
    upon the ground.

They're a little bit rough, I must confess, the most
    of them, at least;
But if you do not hunt a quarrel you can live with
    them in peace;
For if you do, you're sure to rue the day you joined
    their band.
They will follow you up and shoot it out with you
    just man to man.

Did you ever go to a cowboy whenever hungry and
    dry,
Asking for a dollar, and have him you deny?
He'll just pull out his pocket book and hand you a
    note,—
They are the fellows to help you whenever you are
    broke.

Go to their ranches and stay a while, they never ask
a cent;
And when they go to town, their money is freely
spent.
They walk straight up and take a drink, paying for
every one,
And they never ask your pardon for anything
they've done.

When they go to their dances, some dance while
others pat.
They ride their bucking bronchos, and wear their
broad-brimmed hats;
With their California saddles, and their pants stuck
in their boots,
You can hear their spurs a-jingling, and perhaps
some of them shoots.

Come all soft-hearted tenderfeet, if you want to
have some fun;
Go live among the cowboys, they'll show you how
it's done.
They'll treat you like a prince, my boys, about them
there's nothing mean;
But don't try to give them too much advice, for all
of them ain't green.

BUCKING BRONCHO

MY love is a rider, wild bronchos he breaks,
Though he's promised to quit it, just for my
sake.
He ties up one foot, the saddle puts on,
With a swing and a jump he is mounted and gone.

The first time I met him, 'twas early one spring,
Riding a broncho, a high-headed thing.
He tipped me a wink as he gaily did go;
For he wished me to look at his bucking broncho.

The next time I saw him 'twas late in the fall,
Swinging the girls at Tomlinson's ball.
He laughed and he talked as we danced to and fro,
Promised never to ride on another broncho.

He made me some presents, among them a ring;
The return that I made him was a far better thing;
'Twas a young maiden's heart, I'd have you all
know;
He's won it by riding his bucking broncho.

My love has a gun, and that gun he can use,
But he's quit his gun fighting as well as his booze;

And he's sold him his saddle, his spurs, and his rope,
And there's no more cow punching, and that's what I
 hope.

My love has a gun that has gone to the bad,
Which makes poor old Jimmy feel pretty damn sad;
For the gun it shoots high and the gun it shoots low,
And it wobbles about like a bucking broncho.

Now all you young maidens, where'er you reside,
Beware of the cowboy who swings the raw-hide;
He'll court you and pet you and leave you and go
In the spring up the trail on his bucking broncho.

THE PECOS QUEEN

WHERE the Pecos River winds and turns in its
   journey to the sea,
From its white walls of sand and rock striving ever
  to be free,
Near the highest railroad bridge that all these modern times have seen,
Dwells fair young Patty Morehead, the Pecos River
  queen.

She is known by every cowboy on the Pecos River
  wide,
They know full well that she can shoot, that she can
  rope and ride.
She goes to every round-up, every cow work without
  fail,
Looking out for her cattle, branded " walking hog
  on rail."

She made her start in cattle, yes, made it with her
  rope;
Can tie down every maverick before it can strike a
  lope.
She can rope and tie and brand it as quick as any
  man;
She's voted by all cowboys an A-1 top cow hand.

369

The Pecos Queen

Across the Comstock railroad bridge, the highest in
    the West,
Patty rode her horse one day, a lover's heart to test;
For he told her he would gladly risk all dangers for
    her sake —
But the puncher wouldn't follow, so she's still with-
    out a mate.

CHOPO

THROUGH rocky arroyas so dark and so deep,
   Down the sides of the mountains so slippery
      and steep,—
You've good judgment, sure-footed, wherever you
      go,
You're a safety conveyance, my little Chopo.

   Refrain:—
   Chopo, my pony, Chopo, my pride,
   Chopo, my amigo, Chopo I will ride.
   From Mexico's borders 'cross Texas' Llano
   To the salt Pecos River, I ride you, Chopo.

Whether single or double or in the lead of the team,
Over highways or byways or crossing a stream,—
You're always in fix and willing to go,
Whenever you're called on, my chico Chopo.

You're a good roping horse, you were never jerked
      down,
When tied to a steer, you will circle him round;
Let him once cross the string and over he'll go,—
You sabe the business, my cow-horse, Chopo.

Chopo

One day on the Llano a hailstorm began,
The herds were stampeded, the horses all ran,
The lightning it glittered, a cyclone did blow,
But you faced the sweet music, my little Chopo.

TOP HAND

WHILE you're all so frisky I'll sing a little
song,—
Think a little horn of whiskey will help the thing
along?
It's all about the Top Hand, when he busted flat
Bummin' round the town, in his Mexican hat.
He's laid up all winter, and his pocket book is flat,
His clothes are all tatters, but he don't mind that.

See him in town with a crowd that he knows,
Rollin' cigarettes and smokin' through his nose.
First thing he tells you, he owns a certain brand,—
Leads you to think he is a daisy hand;
Next thing he tells you 'bout his trip up the trail,
All the way to Kansas, to finish out his tale.

Put him on a hoss, he's a handy hand to work;
Put him in the brandin'-pen, he's dead sure to shirk.
With his natural leaf tobacco in the pockets of his
vest
He'll tell you his California pants are the best.
He's handled lots of cattle, hasn't any fears,
Can draw his sixty dollars for the balance of his
years.

Put him on herd, he's a-cussin' all day;
Anything he tries, it's sure to get away.

Top Hand

When you have a round-up, he tells it all about
He's goin' to do the cuttin' an' you can't keep him
    out.
If anything goes wrong, he lays it on the screws,
Says the lazy devils were tryin' to take a snooze.

When he meets a greener he ain't afraid to rig,
Stands him on a chuck box and makes him dance a
    jig,—
Waves a loaded cutter, makes him sing and shout,—
He's a regular Ben Thompson when the boss ain't
    about.
When the boss ain't about he leaves his leggins in
    camp,
He swears a man who wears them is worse than a
    tramp.

Says he's not carin' for the wages he earns,
For Dad's rich in Texas,— got wagon loads to burn;
But when he goes to town, he's sure to take it in,
He's always been dreaded wherever he's been.
He rides a fancy horse, he's a favorite man,
Can get more credit than a common waddie can.

When you ship the cattle he's bound to go along
To keep the boss from drinking and see that noth-
    ing's wrong.
Wherever he goes, catch on to his name,
He likes to be called with a handle to his name.
He's always primping with a pocket looking-glass,
From the top to the bottom he's a bold Jackass.

CALIFORNIA TRAIL

L IST all you California boys
    And open wide your ears,
For now we start across the plains
With a herd of mules and steers.
Now, bear in mind before you start,
That you'll eat jerked beef, not ham,
And antelope steak, Oh cuss the stuff!
It often proves a sham.

You cannot find a stick of wood
On all this prairie wide;
Whene'er you eat you've got to stand
Or sit on some old bull hide.
It's fun to cook with buffalo chips
Or mesquite, green as corn,—
If I'd once known what I know now
I'd have gone around Cape Horn.

The women have the hardest time
Who emigrate by land;
For when they cook out in the wind
They're sure to burn their hand.
Then they scold their husbands round,
Get mad and spill the tea,—
I'd have thanked my stars if they'd not come out
Upon this bleak prairie.

Most every night we put out guards
To keep the Indians off.
When night comes round some heads will ache,
And some begin to cough.
To be deprived of help at night,
You know is mighty hard,
But every night there's someone sick
To keep from standing guard.

Then they're always talking of what they've got,
And what they're going to do;
Some will say they're content,
For I've got as much as you.
Others will say, " I'll buy or sell,
I'm damned if I care which."
Others will say, " Boys, buy him out,
For he doesn't own a stitch."

Old raw-hide shoes are hell on corns
While tramping through the sands,
And driving jackass by the tail,—
Damn the overland!
I would as leaf be on a raft at sea
And there at once be lost.
John, let's leave the poor old mule,
We'll never get him across!

BRONC PEELER'S SONG

I'VE been upon the prairie,
   I've been upon the plain,
I've never rid a steam-boat,
Nor a double-cinched-up train.
But I've driv my eight-up to wagon
That were locked three in a row,
And that through blindin' sand storms,
And all kinds of wind and snow.

> Cho: —
> Goodbye, Liza, poor gal,
> Goodbye, Liza Jane,
> Goodbye, Liza, poor gal,
> She died on the plain.

There never was a place I've been
Had any kind of wood.
We burn the roots of bar-grass
And think it's very good.
I've never tasted home bread,
Nor cakes, nor muss like that;
But I know fried dough and beef
Pulled from red-hot tallow fat.

I hate to see the wire fence
'A-closin' up the range;

And all this fillin' in the trail
With people that is strange.
We fellers don't know how to plow,
Nor reap the golden grain;
But to round up steers and brand the cows
To us was allus plain.

So when this blasted country
Is all closed in with wire,
And all the top, as trot grass,
Is burnin' in Sol's fire,
I hope the settlers will be glad
When rain hits the land.
And all us cowdogs are in hell
With a " set " * joined hand in hand.

* " set " means settler.

A DEER HUNT

ONE pleasant summer day it came a storm of
  snow;
I picked my old gun and a-hunting I did go.

I came across a herd of deer and I trailed them
  through the snow,
I trailed them to the mountains where straight up
  they did go.

I trailed them o'er the mountains, I trailed them to
  the brim,
And I trailed them to the waters where they jumped
  in to swim.

I cocked both my pistols and under water went,—
To kill the fattest of them deer, that was my whole
  intent.

While I was under water five hundred feet or more
I fired both my pistols; like cannons did they roar.

I picked up my venison and out of water came,—
To kill the balance of them deer, I thought it would
  be fun.

So I bent my gun in circles and fired round a hill.
And, out of three or four deer, ten thousand I did
    kill.

Then I picked up my venison and on my back I tied
And as the sun came passing by I hopped up there
    to ride.

The sun she carried me o'er the globe, so merrily I
    did roam
That in four and twenty hours I landed safe at home.

And the money I received for my venison and skin,
I taken it all to the barn door and it would not all
    go in.

And if you doubt the truth of this I tell you how to
    know:
Just take my trail and go my rounds, as I did, long
    ago.

WINDY BILL

WINDY BILL was a Texas man,—
    Well, he could rope, you bet.
He swore the steer he couldn't tie,—
Well, he hadn't found him yet.
But the boys they knew of an old black steer,
A sort of an old outlaw
That ran down in the malpais
At the foot of a rocky draw.

This old black steer had stood his ground
With punchers from everywhere;
So they bet old Bill at two to one
That he couldn't quite get there.
Then Bill brought out his old gray hoss,
His withers and back were raw,
And prepared to tackle the big black brute
That ran down in the draw.

With his brazen bit and his Sam Stack tree
His chaps and taps to boot,
And his old maguey tied hard and fast,
Bill swore he'd get the brute.
Now, first Bill sort of sauntered round
Old Blackie began to paw,
Then threw his tail straight in the air
And went driftin' down the draw.

Windy Bill

The old gray plug flew after him,
For he'd been eatin' corn;
And Bill, he piled his old maguey
Right round old Blackie's horns.
The old gray hoss he stopped right still;
The cinches broke like straw,
And the old maguey and the Sam Stack tree
Went driftin' down the draw.

Bill, he lit in a flint rock pile,
His face and hands were scratched.
He said he thought he could rope a snake
But he guessed he'd met his match.
He paid his bets like a little man
Without a bit of jaw,
And lowed old Blackie was the boss
Of anything in the draw.

There's a moral to my story, boys,
And that you all must see.
Whenever you go to tie a snake,***
Don't tie it to your tree;
But take your dolly welters *
'Cordin' to California law,
And you'll never see your old rim-fire **
Go drifting down the draw.

*** snake, bad steer.
* Dolly welter, rope tied all around the saddle.
** rim-fire saddle, without flank girth.

WILD ROVERS

COME all you wild rovers
       And listen to me
While I retail to you
My sad history.
I'm a man of experience
Your favors to gain,
Oh, love has been the ruin
Of many a poor man.

When you are single
And living at your ease
You can roam this world over
And do as you please;
You can roam this world over
And go where you will
And slyly kiss a pretty girl
And be your own still.

But when you are married
And living with your wife,
You've lost all the joys
And comforts of life.
Your wife she will scold you,
Your children will cry,

And that will make papa
Look withered and dry.

You can't step aside, boys,
To speak to a friend
Without your wife at your elbow
Saying, " What does this mean? "
Your wife, she will scold
And there is sad news.
Dear boys, take warning;
'Tis a life to refuse.

If you chance to be riding
Along the highway
And meet a fair maiden,
A lady so gay,
With red, rosy cheeks
And sparkling blue eyes,—
Oh, heavens! what a tumult
In your bosom will rise!

One more request, boys,
Before we must part:
Don't place your affections
On a charming sweetheart;
She'll dance before you
Your favors to gain.
Oh, turn your back on them
With scorn and disdain!

Wild Rovers

Come close to the bar, boys,
We'll drink all around.
We'll drink to the pure,
If any be found;
We'll drink to the single,
For I wish them success;
Likewise to the married,
For I wish them no less.

LIFE IN A HALF-BREED SHACK

'TIS life in a half-breed shack,
   The rain comes pouring down;
" Drip " drops the mud through the roof,
And the wind comes through the wall.
A tenderfoot cursed his luck
And feebly cried out " yah! "

   Refrain:
   Yah!   Yah!   I want to go home to my ma!
   Yah!   Yah! this bloomin' country's a fraud!
   Yah!   Yah!   I want to go home to my ma!

He tries to kindle a fire
When it's forty-five below;
He aims to chop at a log
And amputates his toe;
He hobbles back to the shack
And feebly cries out " yah "!

He gets on a bucking cayuse
And thinks to flourish around,
But the buzzard-head takes to bucking
And lays him flat out on the ground.
As he picks himself up with a curse,
He feebly cries out " yah "!

He buys all the town lots he can get
In the wrong end of Calgary,
And he waits and he waits for the boom
Until he's dead broke like me.
He couldn't get any tick
So he feebly cries out " yah "!

He couldn't do any work
And he wouldn't know how if he could;
So the police run him for a vag
And set him to bucking wood.
As he sits in the guard room cell,
He feebly cries out " yah "!

Come all ye tenderfeet
And listen to what I say,
If you can't get a government job
You had better remain where you be.
Then you won't curse your luck
And cry out feebly " yah "!

THE ROAD TO COOK'S PEAK

IF you'll listen a while I'll sing you a song,
   And as it is short it won't take me long.
There are some things of which I will speak
Concerning the stage on the road to Cook's Peak.
On the road to Cook's Peak,—
On the road to Cook's Peak,—
Concerning the stage on the road to Cook's Peak.

It was in the morning at eight-forty-five,
I was hooking up all ready to drive
Out where the miners for minerals seek,
With two little mules on the road to Cook's Peak —
On the road to Cook's Peak,—
On the road to Cook's Peak,—
With two little mules on the road to Cook's Peak.

With my two little mules I jog along
And try to cheer them with ditty and song;
O'er the wide prairie where coyotes sneak,
While driving the stage on the road to Cook's Peak.
On the road to Cook's Peak,—
On the road to Cook's Peak,—
While driving the stage on the road to Cook's Peak.

Sometimes I have to haul heavy freight,
Then it is I get home very late.

The Road to Cook's Peak

In rain or shine, six days in the week,
'Tis the same little mules on the road to Cook's
    Peak.
On the road to Cook's Peak,—
On the road to Cook's Peak,—
'Tis the same little mules on the road to Cook's
    Peak.

And when with the driving of stage I am through
I will to my two little mules bid adieu.
And hope that those creatures, so gentle and meek,
Will have a good friend on the road to Cook's Peak.
On the road to Cook's Peak,—
On the road to Cook's Peak,—
Will have a good friend on the road to Cook's Peak.

Now all kind friends that travel about,
Come take a trip on the Wallis stage route.
With a plenty of grit, they never get weak,—
Those two little mules on the road to Cook's Peak.
On the road to Cook's Peak,—
On the road to Cook's Peak,—
Those two little mules on the road to Cook's Peak.

ARAPHOE, OR BUCKSKIN JOE

'TWAS a calm and peaceful evening in a camp
    called Araphoe,
And the whiskey was a running with a soft and gentle
    flow,
The music was a-ringing in a dance hall cross the
    way,
And the dancers was a-swinging just as close as they
    could lay.

People gathered round the tables, a-betting with
    their wealth,
And near by stood a stranger who had come there
    for his health.
He was a peaceful little stranger though he seemed
    to be unstrung;
For just before he'd left his home he'd separated
    with one lung.

Nearby at a table sat a man named Hankey Dean,
A tougher man says Hankey, buckskin chaps had
    never seen.
But Hankey was a gambler and he was plum sure to
    lose;
For he had just departed with a sun-dried stack of
    blues.

He rose from the table, on the floor his last chip
    flung,
And cast his fiery glimmers on the man with just one
    lung.
" No wonder I've been losing every bet I made to-
    night
When a sucker and a tenderfoot was between me and
    the light.

Look here, little stranger, do you know who I am? "
" Yes, and I don't care a copper colored damn."
The dealers stopped their dealing and the players
    held their breath;
For words like those to Hankey were a sudden flirt
    with death.

" Listen, gentle stranger, I'll read my pedigree:
I'm known on handling tenderfeet and worser men
    than thee;
The lions on the mountains, I've drove them to their
    lairs;
The wild-cats are my playmates, and I've wrestled
    grizzly bears;

" Why, the centipedes can't mar my tough old hide,
And rattle snakes have bit me and crawled off and
    died.
I'm as wild as the horse that roams the range;
The moss grows on my teeth and wild blood flows
    through my veins.

" I'm wild and woolly and full of fleas
And never curried below the knees.
Now, little stranger, if you'll give me your address,—
How would you like to go, by fast mail or express? "

The little stranger who was leaning on the door
Picked up a hand of playing cards that were scattered
  on the floor.
Picking out the five of spades, he pinned it to the
  door
And then stepped back some twenty paces or more.

He pulled out his life-preserver, and with a " one,
  two, three, four,"
Blotted out a spot with every shot;
For he had traveled with a circus and was a fancy
  pistol shot.
" I have one more left, kind sir, if you wish to call
  the play."

Then Hanke stepped up to the stranger and made a
  neat apology,
" Why, the lions in the mountains,— that was nothing but a joke.
Never mind about the extra, you are a bad shooting
  man,
And I'm a meek little child and as harmless as a
  lamb."

ROUNDED UP IN GLORY

I HAVE been thinking to-day,
  As my thoughts began to stray,
Of your memory to me worth more than gold.
As you ride across the plain,
'Mid the sunshine and the rain,—
You will be rounded up in glory bye and bye

  Chorus:
    You will be rounded up in glory bye and bye,
    You will be rounded up in glory bye and bye,
    When the milling time is o'er
    And you will stampede no more,
    When he rounds you up within the Master's
      fold.

As you ride across the plain
With the cowboys that have fame,
And the storms and the lightning flash by.
We shall meet to part no more
Upon the golden shore
When he rounds us up in glory bye and bye.

May we lift our voices high
To that sweet bye and bye,

And be known by the brand of the Lord;
For his property we are,
And he will know us from afar
When he rounds us up in glory bye and bye.

THE DRUNKARD'S HELL

IT was on a cold and stormy night
I saw and heard an awful sight;
The lightning flashed and thunder rolled
Around my poor benighted soul.

I thought I heard a mournful sound
Among the groans still lower down,
That awful sight no tongue can tell
Is this,— the place called Drunkard's Hell.

I thought I saw the gulf below
Where all the dying drunkards go.
I raised my hand and sad to tell
It was the place called Drunkard's Hell.

I traveled on and got there at last
And started to take a social glass;
But every time I started,— well,
I thought about the Drunkard's Hell.

I dashed it down to leave that place
And started to seek redeeming grace.
I felt like Paul, at once I'd pray
Till all my sins were washed away.

The Drunkard's Hell

I then went home to change my life
And see my long neglected wife.
I found her weeping o'er the bed
Because her infant babe was dead.

I told her not to mourn and weep
Because her babe had gone to sleep;
Its happy soul had fled away
To dwell with Christ till endless day.

I taken her by her pale white hand,
She was so weak she could not stand;
I laid her down and breathed a prayer
That God might bless and save her there.

I then went to the Temperance hall
And taken a pledge among them all.
They taken me in with a willing hand
And taken me in as a temperance man.

So seven long years have passed away
Since first I bowed my knees to pray;
So now I live a sober life
With a happy home and a loving wife.

RAMBLING BOY

I AM a wild and roving lad,
   A wild and rambling lad I'll be;
For I do love a little girl
And she does love me.

" O Willie, O Willie, I love you so,
I love you more than I do know;
And if my tongue could tell you so
I'd give the world to let you know."

When Julia's old father came this to know,—
That Julia and Willie were loving so,—
He ripped and swore among them all,
And swore he'd use a cannon ball.

She wrote Willie a letter with her right hand
And sent it to him in the western land.
" Oh, read these lines, sweet William dear.
For this is the last of me you will hear."

He read those lines while he wept and cried,
" Ten thousand times I wish I had died "
He read those lines while he wept and said,
" Ten thousand times I wish I were dead."

When her old father came home that night
He called for Julia, his heart's delight,
He ran up stairs and her door he broke
And found her hanging by her own bed rope.

And with his knife he cut her down,
And in her bosom this note he found
Saying, " Dig my grave both deep and wide
And bury sweet Willie by my side."

They dug her grave both deep and wide
And buried sweet Willie by her side;
And on her grave set a turtle dove
To show the world they died for love.

BRIGHAM YOUNG. I.

I'LL sing you a song that has often been sung
    About an old Mormon they called Brigham
      Young.
Of wives he had many who were strong in the lungs,
Which Brigham found out by the length of their
      tongues.
Ri tu ral, lol, lu ral.

Oh, sad was the life of a Mormon to lead,
Yet Brigham adhered all his life to his creed.
He said 'twas such fun, and true, without doubt,
To see the young wives knock the old ones about.
Ri tu ral, lol, lu ral.

One day as old Brigham sat down to his dinner
He saw a young wife who was not getting thinner;
When the elders cried out, one after the other,
By the holy, she wants to go home to her mother.
Ri tu ral, lol, lu ral.

Old Brigham replied, which can't be denied,
He couldn't afford to lose such a bride.
Then do not be jealous but banish your fears;
For the tree is well known by the fruit that it bears.
Ri tu ral, lol, lu ral.

Brigham Young. I.

Thät I love one and all you very well know,
Then do not provoke me or my anger will show.
What must be our fate if found here in a row,
If Uncle Sam comes with his row-de-dow-dow.
Ri tu ral, lol, lu ral.

Then cease all your quarrels and do not despair,
To meet Uncle Sam I will quickly prepare.
Hark! I hear Yankee Doodle played over the hills!
Ah! here's the enemy with their powder and pills.
Ri tu ral, lol, lu ral.

BRIGHAM YOUNG. II.

NOW Brigham Young is a Mormon bold,
    And a leader of the roaring rams,
And shepherd of a lot of fine tub sheep
And a lot of pretty little lambs.
Oh, he lives with his five and forty wives,
In the city of the Great Salt Lake,
Where they breed and swarm like hens on a farm
And cackle like ducks to a drake.

    Chorus: —

    Oh Brigham, Brigham Young,
    It's a miracle how you survive,
    With your roaring rams and your pretty little
        lambs
    And your five and forty wives.

Number forty-five is about sixteen,
Number one is sixty and three;
And they make such a riot, how he keeps them quiet
Is a downright mystery to me.
For they clatter and they chaw and they jaw, jaw,
    jaw,
And each has a different desire;
It would aid the renown of the best shop in town
To supply them with half they desire.

401

Now, Brigham Young was a stout man once,
And now he is thin and old;
And I am sorry to state he is bald on the pate,
Which once had a covering of gold.
For his oldest wives won't have white wool,
And his young ones won't have red,
So, with tearing it out, and taking turn about,
They have torn all the hair off his head.

Now, the oldest wives sing songs all day,
And the young ones all sing songs;
And amongst such a crowd he has it pretty loud,—
They're as noisy as Chinese gongs.
And when they advance for a Mormon dance
He is filled with the direst alarms;
For they are sure to end the night in a tabernacle
      fight
To see who has the fairest charms.

Now, if any man here envies Brigham Young
Let him go to the Great Salt Lake;
And if he has the leisure to enjoy his pleasure,
He'll find it a great mistake.
One wife at a time, so says my rhyme,
Is enough,— there's no denial; —
So, before you strive to be lord of forty-five,
Take two for a month on trial.

THE OLD GRAY MULE

I AM an old man some sixty years old
And that you can plain-li see,
But when I was a young man ten years old
They made a stable boy of me.

I have seen the fastest horses
That made the fastest time,
But I never saw one in all my life
Like that old gray mule of mine.

On a Sunday morn I dress myself,
A-goin' out to ride;
Now, my old mule is as gray as a bird,
Then he is full of his pride.

He never runs away with you,
Never cuts up any shine;
For the only friend I have on earth
Is this old gray mule of mine.

Now my old gray mule is dead and gone,
Gone to join the heavenly band,
With silver shoes upon his feet
To dance on the golden strand.

THE FOOLS OF FORTY-NINE

WHEN gold was found in forty-eight the people thought 'twas gas,
And some were fools enough to think the lumps were
only brass.
But soon they all were satisfied and started off to
mine;
They bought their ships, came round the Horn, in
the days of forty-nine.

Refrain:
Then they thought of what they'd been told
When they started after gold,—
That they never in the world would make a pile.

The people all were crazy then, they didn't know
what to do.
They sold their farms for just enough to pay their
passage through.
They bid their friends a long farewell, said, " Dear
wife, don't you cry,
I'll send you home the yellow lumps a piano for to
buy."

The poor, the old, and the rotten scows were ad-
vertised to sail

From New Orleans with passengers, but they must
    pump and bail.
The ships were crowded more than full, and some
    hung on behind,
And others dived off from the wharf and swam till
    they were blind.

With rusty pork and stinking beef and rotten,
    wormy bread!
The captains, too, that never were up as high as the
    main mast head!
The steerage passengers would rave and swear that
    they'd paid their passage
And wanted something more to eat beside bologna
    sausage.

They then began to cross the plain with oxen, hol-
    lowing " haw."
And steamers then began to run as far as Panama.
And there for months the people staid, that started
    after gold,
And some returned disgusted with the lies that had
    been told.

The people died on every route, they sickened and
    died like sheep;
And those at sea before they died were launched into
    the deep;

And those that died while crossing the plains fared
    not so well as that,
For a hole was dug and they thrown in along the
    miserable Platte.

The ships at last began to arrive and the people be-
    gan to inquire.
They say that flour is a dollar a pound, do you think
    it will be any higher?
And to carry their blankets and sleep outdoors, it
    seemed so very droll!
Both tired and mad, without a cent, they damned the
    lousy hole.

A RIPPING TRIP *

Y OU go aboard a leaky boat
   And sail for San Francisco,
You've got to pump to keep her afloat,
You've got that, by jingo!
The engine soon begins to squeak,
But nary a thing to oil her;
Impossible to stop the leak,—
Rip, goes the boiler.

The captain on the promenade
Looking very savage;
Steward and the cabin maid
Fightin' 'bout the cabbage;
All about the cabin floor
Passengers lie sea-sick;
Steamer bound to go ashore,—
Rip, goes the physic.

Pork and beans they can't afford,
The second cabin passengers;
The cook has tumbled overboard
With fifty pounds of sassengers;

* To tune of *Pop Goes the Weasel.*

A Ripping Trip

The engineer, a little tight,
Bragging on the Mail Line,
Finally gets into a fight,—
Rip, goes the engine.

THE HAPPY MINER

I'M a happy miner,
　　I love to sing and dance.
I wonder what my love would say
If she could see my pants
With canvas patches on my knees
And one upon the stern?
I'll wear them when I'm digging here
And home when I return.

　　Refrain:
　　So I get in a jovial way,
　　I spend my money free.
　　And I've got plenty!
　　Will you drink lager beer with me?

She writes about her poodle dog;
But never thinks to say,
"Oh, do come home, my honey dear,
I'm pining all away."
I'll write her half a letter,
Then give the ink a tip.
If that don't bring her to her milk
I'll coolly let her rip.

They wish to know if I can cook
And what I have to eat,

And tell me should I take a cold
Be sure and soak my feet.
But when they talk of cooking
I'm mighty hard to beat,
I've made ten thousand loaves of bread
The devil couldn't eat.

I like a lazy partner
So I can take my ease,
Lay down and talk of golden home,
As happy as you please;
Without a thing to eat or drink,
Away from care and grief,—
I'm fat and sassy, ragged, too,
And tough as Spanish beef.

No matter whether rich or poor,
I'm happy as a clam.
I wish my friends at home could look
And see me as I am.
With woolen shirt and rubber boots,
In mud up to my knees,
And lice as large as chilli beans
Fighting with the fleas.

I'll mine for half an ounce a day,
Perhaps a little less;
But when it comes to China pay
I cannot stand the press.
Like thousands there, I'll make a pile,
If I make one at all,
About the time the allied forces
Take Sepasterpol.

THE CALIFORNIA STAGE COMPANY

THERE'S no respect for youth or age
   On board the California stage,
But pull and haul about the seats
As bed-bugs do about the sheets.

   Refrain:
   They started as a thieving line
   In eighteen hundred and forty-nine;
   All opposition they defy,
   So the people must root hog or die.

You're crowded in with Chinamen,
As fattening hogs are in a pen;
And what will more a man provoke
Is musty plug tobacco smoke.

The ladies are compelled to sit
With dresses in tobacco spit;
The gentlemen don't seem to care,
But talk on politics and swear.

The dust is deep in summer time,
The mountains very hard to climb,
And drivers often stop and yell,
" Get out, all hands, and push up hill."

The drivers, when they feel inclined,
Will have you walking on behind,
And on your shoulders lug a pole
To help them out some muddy hole.

They promise when your fare you pay,
" You'll have to walk but half the way ";
Then add aside, with cunning laugh,
" You'll have to push the other half."

NEW NATIONAL ANTHEM

MY country, 'tis of thee,
    Land where things used to be
So cheap, we croak.
Land of the mavericks,
Land of the puncher's tricks,
Thy culture-inroad pricks
The hide of this peeler-bloke.

Some of the punchers swear
That what they eat and wear
Takes all their calves.
Others vow that they
Eat only once a day
Jerked beef and prairie hay
Washed down with tallow salves.

These salty-dogs ** but crave
To pull them out the grave
Just one Kiowa spur.
They know they still will dine
On flesh and beef the time;
But give us, Lord divine,
One " hen-fruit stir." *

** Cowboy Dude.
* Pancake.

Our father's land, with thee,
Best trails of liberty,
We chose to stop.
We don't exactly like
So soon to henceward hike,
But hell, we'll take the pike
If this don't stop.